AF326853

"IN A MOMENT, IN THE TWINKLING OF AN EYE,
AT THE LAST TRUMPET."

THE WHOLE TRUTH ABOUT THE RAPTURE

WRITTEN BY

THOMAS ARMENTROUT

First print edition February 2022

ISBN: 978-0-578-38544-0 (PAPERBACK)

Scriptures used from NKJV, NIV, and KJV Bibles

Made and Printed in the USA

Acknowledgements

First, I want to thank the Lord for this message and this book, the dream that inspired it, and for guiding me through the whole process.

I want to thank my son Jacob who did a brilliant job transforming a very large word document that was in need of editing into the very first draft of the book, which I took as a clear sign from the Lord that He wanted this message to be a book. After adding some additional chapters, Jacob not only published the book but also created the website and videos.

Jacob and his wife Sophia are now the official publishers for Armed in Christ Ministries, which will be releasing more books in the future.

CONTENTS

INTRODUCTION

My name is Tom Armentrout, and I want to present to you a case study I have written to reveal *The Whole Truth About the Rapture*. You will soon understand why I say *The Whole Truth* because in this investigation, I will attempt to uncover all the facts that are in Scripture of what I believe to be a very important message.

I will give you a little history on how this all began. Many years ago, back in the late '80s and early '90s, I had a strong interest in prophecy, and at that time, so did many others, and there were several popular books and movies that I think helped popularize it among many Christians then. Most of the teachings at that time revolved around a popular subject called *the Rapture*. One night, back in the early '90s, I had what I believed to be a dream from the Lord that challenged my beliefs concerning the *Rapture* and *Prophecy*. The dream did not change my beliefs about the Rapture but led me to do a thorough investigation of Scripture for the Truth about the Rapture. I believe the Lord guided me in this research, and I am now convinced that Scripture paints a clear picture of this Truth and confirmed what the Lord showed me in the dream. Having sought the Lord on how to best present this research, I believe He has directed me to present this as a complete series of questions covering as much as possible, everything that Scripture has to teach us on this subject, staying focused on this message.

There are ten major questions we are going to cover in this study, and they will often lead to other questions to which we will answer as well.

COMMENTS

In this study we will be learning the following answers:

—   That there is, for certain, a Rapture in Scripture.

—   What the Rapture is.

—   Who will be in the Rapture.

—   Why there must be a Rapture in the first place.

—   Where the Rapture takes place.

—   If there is only one Rapture.

—   When the Rapture happens according to Scripture. This is probably the most important question for many but by answering the previous questions we begin to see the bigger picture, and when we fit all the answers from Scripture together with the answers to our question of when the Rapture takes place, we will begin to see the whole picture that Scripture paints.

—   Why the Rapture is when it is.

—   Why the Truth about the Rapture is important.

What happens after the Rapture takes place.

THE WHOLE TRUTH ABOUT THE RAPTURE

QUESTION 1

IS THERE A RAPTURE?

The word Rapture is not in the Bible, but has become a popular term used to describe the events found in *1 Thessalonians 4:16-17*. Let's read these verses.

I THESSALONIANS 4:16-17 (NKJV)
16 For the Lord Himself will descend from heaven with a shout, with the voice of an archangel, and with the trumpet of God. And the dead in Christ will rise first.
17 Then we who are alive and remain shall be caught up together with them in the clouds to meet the Lord in the air. And thus we shall always be with the Lord.

The word Rapture has a similar meaning to the words "caught up" in *verse 17*, which has become accepted to use instead of the words "caught up." It is more than just a word replacement, but now an accepted term used to express the meaning of the event described in *verse 17*, *"we who are alive and remain shall be caught up together with them in the clouds to meet the Lord in the air."*

So, to summarize this, the term Rapture has come to mean the catching up of the saints who are still alive and remain when the Lord returns. There is a second set of verses that also describe the Rapture in *1 Corinthians*. Let's take a look at them as well.

I CORINTHIANS 15:51-52 (NKJV)
51 Behold, I tell you a mystery: We shall not all sleep, but we shall all be changed—
52 in a moment, in the twinkling of an eye, at the last

trumpet. For the trumpet will sound, and the dead will be raised incorruptible, and we shall be changed.

We know that the word "sleep" here means those who have died because *verse 52* says that the dead shall be raised. It confirms *"We shall not all sleep"* means that we will not all die, which agrees with the previous Rapture verse in *1 Thessalonians 4:17* that states *"we who are alive and remain shall be caught up."* Both passages teach that some of us will still be alive when this event occurs.

To answer the question—*Is there a Rapture?* Even though the word Rapture is not used in the Bible, the event it has become known to represent does exist. The answer is yes, there is a Rapture.

QUESTION 2

WHAT IS THE RAPTURE?

To answer this question, we will continue to examine the two Rapture passages and let them provide the answer to the question.

I THESSALONIANS 4:16-17 (NKJV)

¹⁶ For the Lord Himself will descend from heaven with a shout, with the voice of an archangel, and with the trumpet of God. And the dead in Christ will rise first.
¹⁷ Then we who are alive and remain shall be caught up together with them in the clouds to meet the Lord in the air. And thus we shall always be with the Lord.

The first answer to our question in this passage is that the Rapture is at the coming of the Lord. The next answer is that the Rapture is included with the Resurrection and is part of the same event. Let's look at the second passage of Scripture written about the Rapture for more answers to this question.

I CORINTHIANS 15:51-52 (NKJV)

⁵¹ Behold, I tell you a mystery: We shall not all sleep, but we shall all be changed—
⁵² in a moment, in the twinkling of an eye, at the last trumpet. For the trumpet will sound, and the dead will be raised incorruptible, and we shall be changed.

In this passage, the Apostle Paul says he is telling a mystery. Why is it a mystery? Until Paul wrote the two letters that introduced the Rapture to the Churches they had no knowledge of the Rapture, only the Resurrection, which assumes everybody would be dead at the time of the Resurrection. What makes this a mystery is that Paul revealed something that was unknown to the Church until he introduced it in the two passages of Scripture that we are now studying, and that is, not all Christians are going to be dead at the time of the Resurrection. So, another answer to the question; it is a mystery revealed to the Church.

There is one more answer to the question of what the Rapture is that we should look at, and it is not found directly in the Rapture passages, but it is in the same chapter and is what leads up to Paul introducing the Rapture to the Church. It is the *Hope of All Saints*. This hope is also known as the *Blessed Hope* and is found in the book of *Titus*.

TITUS 2:13 (NKJV)
13 looking for the blessed Hope and glorious appearing of our great God and Savior Jesus Christ,

Since the Apostle Paul says we are looking for the Blessed Hope and the coming of the Lord, he is saying the Blessed Hope is going to happen at the coming of the Lord. Therefore, it is something additional that is going to take place at the coming of the Lord. With that, let's look at the verses in the chapter that lead up to the Rapture in *1 Thessalonians 4* and see what they tell us about this hope.

1 THESSALONIANS 4:13-15 (NKJV)
13 But I do not want you to be ignorant, brethren, concerning those who have fallen asleep, lest you sorrow as others who have no hope.
14 For if we believe that Jesus died and rose again, even so God will bring with Him those who sleep in Jesus.
15 For this we say to you by the word of the Lord, that we who are alive and remain until the coming of the Lord will by no means precede those who are asleep.

The Apostle Paul is describing that the hope of the believers is unlike that of non-believers who have no hope of seeing their loved ones again. The believers will see their loved ones again at the Resurrection when Jesus comes. He goes on to say in *verse 15* that the saints who are alive and remain until the coming of the Lord will not rise to meet the Lord until after those who have died are resurrected first. This clearly is giving a precedence to those who have died over those who are still alive and are caught up to meet them and the Lord at His coming. This is described in the next two verses of this chapter and are the Rapture verses.

I THESSALONIANS 4:16-17 (NKJV)

[16] For the Lord Himself will descend from heaven with a shout, with the voice of an archangel, and with the trumpet of God. And the dead in Christ will rise first.
[17] Then we who are alive and remain shall be caught up together with them in the clouds to meet the Lord in the air. And thus we shall always be with the Lord.

To clarify, the Apostle Paul is describing that the hope of all saints is the Resurrection, and that they will be able to see their loved ones again. There are other Scriptures that also declare that the hope of the believer is the Resurrection found in *Acts 24*.

ACTS 24:14-15 (NKJV)

[14] I believe everything that is in accordance with the Law and that is written in the Prophets,
[15] I have Hope in God, which they themselves also accept, that there will be a Resurrection of the dead, both of the just and the unjust.

The Apostle Paul says here that his Hope in God is *"that there will be a Resurrection of the dead."* This Scripture shows that the hope of the believers is the Resurrection, which make sense. Remember, we just learned that the Rapture is a mystery that the Apostle Paul revealed to the Churches. Until he revealed the Rapture, the saints did not know anyone would be alive at the time of the Resurrection, so the Resurrection alone would have been the hope of all saints. The Rapture by itself, since Scripture defines the Resurrection as the Blessed Hope, may not appropriately be called the Blessed Hope, but since the Rapture is not a lone event but instead included with the Resurrection at the coming of the Lord, I believe it is appropriate to call the Rapture the Blessed Hope also. With that said, a final answer to the question, it is the Blessed Hope of the saints.

The answers to the question—*What is the Rapture?*

1. It is the catching up of the saints who are still alive and remain.
2. It is an event at the coming of the Lord.
3. It is part of the Resurrection of the saints.
4. It is a mystery revealed to the Church.
5. It is the hope of the believers still alive when the Lord returns.

Since the Resurrection occurs first, until the Rapture was revealed, it was all that was known. It was the main event that the saints had been waiting for. I think it is fair to say that the Rapture is not just included with the Resurrection but is part of the Resurrection.

QUESTION 3

WHO IS IN THE RAPTURE?

Again, we will look to our two Rapture passages to answer this question.

I THESSALONIANS 4:16-17 (NKJV)
16 For the Lord Himself will descend from heaven with a shout, with the voice of an archangel, and with the trumpet of God. And the dead in Christ will rise first.
17 Then we who are alive and remain shall be caught up together with them in the clouds to meet the Lord in the air. And thus we shall always be with the Lord.

Notice it says, *"the dead in Christ will rise first."* Since this Resurrection of the dead is for those in Christ, the Rapture being part of the same event is also going to be for those in Christ. This event includes everyone who has died in Christ, and everyone left alive in Christ, so it is for everyone in Christ. All God's people from all the dispensations. The second Rapture passage confirms this as well.

I CORINTHIANS 15:51-52 (NKJV)
51 Behold, I tell you a mystery: We shall not all sleep, but we shall all be changed—
52 in a moment, in the twinkling of an eye, at the last trumpet. For the trumpet will sound, and the dead will be raised incorruptible, and we shall be changed.

As we have learned, the Rapture is a mystery that reveals we will not all sleep, meaning die, but the rest of the verse says we shall all be changed. All, meaning everyone who is in Christ, as stated *in 1*

Thessalonians 4:16-17. Are there any other passages of Scripture that says all the saints will be included in this event? Yes, in *John 5.*

JOHN 5:28-29 (NKJV)

28 Do not marvel at this; for the hour is coming in which all who are in the graves will hear His voice

29 and come forth—those who have done good, to the Resurrection of Life, and those who have done evil, to the Resurrection of Condemnation.

Jesus, in this passage, says all who are in the graves will be resurrected in one of the two Resurrections. This passage is very clear, everyone who dies will be in one of these two Resurrections. The Resurrection of Life or the Resurrection of Condemnation. This passage does not mention those left alive, but the verses in *1 Thessalonians 4* are clear, those left alive will be caught up together with those being resurrected in the Resurrection of Life, which is for those in Christ.

Summing this all up; after reviewing the Rapture verses and looking at what Jesus said about the Resurrections, we find the answer to the question—*Who is in the Rapture?* Everyone who is in Christ and still on the earth when the Lord comes, and just before them, everyone who has died in Christ. Everyone in Christ will be gathered to Him when He comes.

QUESTION 4

WHY IS THERE A RAPTURE?

As with previous questions, we will start with the Rapture passages to answer this question.

I CORINTHIANS 15:51-52 (NKJV)

51 Behold, I tell you a mystery: We shall not all sleep, but we shall all be changed—

52 in a moment, in the twinkling of an eye, at the last trumpet. For the trumpet will sound, and the dead will be raised incorruptible, and we shall be changed.

I THESSALONIANS 4:16-17 (NKJV)

16 For the Lord Himself will descend from heaven with a shout, with the voice of an archangel, and with the trumpet of God. And the dead in Christ will rise first.

17 Then we who are alive and remain shall be caught up together with them in the clouds to meet the Lord in the air. And thus we shall always be with the Lord.

In a previous question, we learned that the Apostle Paul revealed the Rapture to the Church as a mystery, and it was a mystery because until the Apostle Paul revealed that there will be a Rapture of the saints still alive at the Resurrection, the Church only knew about the Resurrection, and they would have had no way of knowing that the saints will still be alive at the Resurrection. That gives us one reason why there is a Rapture, because the saints will still be alive at the time of the Resurrection and the coming of the Lord. This creates another important question—Why are the saints that are still alive caught up with the saints in the Resurrection? Since the original event known to the saints was the Resurrection, studying the Scriptures on the Resurrection should answer this new question. We will start with Jesus' teachings about the Resurrection.

JOHN 5:28-29 (NKJV)
²⁸ Do not marvel at this; for the hour is coming in which all who are in the graves will hear His voice
²⁹ and come forth—those who have done good, to the Resurrection of Life, and those who have done evil, to the Resurrection of Condemnation.

Jesus says those who have done good will be in the Resurrection of Life, and those who have done evil will be in the Resurrection of Condemnation. The fact that these Resurrections are identified by those who have done good and those who have done evil, with those who have done good receiving life and those who have done evil receiving condemnation, it reveals that these Resurrections are *judgments of the dead*. Further study of the Resurrections will confirm and expound on this. *Revelation 20* has one of the most detailed accounts of the Resurrections.

REVELATION 20:4-6 (NKJV)
⁴ And I saw thrones, and they sat on them, and judgment was committed to them. Then I saw the souls of those who had been beheaded for their witness to Jesus and for the word of God, who had not worshiped the beast or his image, and had not received his mark on their foreheads or on their hands. And they lived and reigned with Christ for a thousand years.
⁵ But the rest of the dead did not live again until the thousand years were finished. This is the first Resurrection.
⁶ Blessed and holy is he who has part in the first Resurrection. Over such the second death has no power, but they shall be priests of God and of Christ and shall reign with Him a thousand years.

This passage is describing the first Resurrection, which is the Resurrection of the saints, and since the Rapture is part of the Resurrection of the saints, the Rapture is part of the first Resurrection. The first thing this passage says is *"And I saw thrones, and they sat on*

them, and judgment was committed to them," giving further evidence of what we learned from the previous passage about the Resurrections taught by Jesus, and that is the Resurrections are judgments of the dead. *Verses 7-10* describe when the thousand years have ended and continues with the description of the Resurrection of the ungodly in *verses 11-15.* We will pick up there and read about that Resurrection next.

REVELATION 20:11-15 (NKJV)

11 Then I saw a great white throne and Him who sat on it, from whose face the earth and the heaven fled away. And there was found no place for them.

12 And I saw the dead, small and great, standing before God, and books were opened. And another book was opened, which is the Book of Life. And the dead were judged according to their works, by the things which were written in the books.

13 The sea gave up the dead who were in it, and Death and Hades delivered up the dead who were in them. And they were judged, each one according to his works.

14 Then Death and Hades were cast into the lake of fire. This is the second death.

15 And anyone not found written in the Book of Life was cast into the lake of fire.

This passage describes God sitting on a great white throne judging the ungodly dead that have been resurrected, and they are judged according to their works, agreeing with what Jesus taught that those who have done evil will be in the Resurrection of Condemnation. As we can see, this passage in Revelation confirms that the Resurrections are judgements. We will soon see why this is important to answering our question of why the saints are still alive and have to be Raptured at the Lord's return and the Resurrection. *Revelation 11:18* is the next Scripture verse we will look at on the Resurrection.

REVELATION 11:18 (NKJV)

18 The nations were angry, and Your wrath has come,
And the time of the dead, that they should be judged,
And that You should reward Your servants the prophets
and the saints, And those who fear Your name, small and

great, And should destroy those who destroy the earth."

This verse declares that this Resurrection of the dead is a judgement for His servants and prophets, and it is a judgement of reward, not punishment. As we read on concerning the Resurrection of the saints in *Revelation 20:6, "Blessed and holy is he who has part in the first Resurrection."* Scripture is painting a picture here that the Resurrection of the saints is not only the Resurrection of Life, but also the time of reward and blessing. Scripture has more to say about this so let's continue to study this.

LUKE 14:13-14 (NKJV)

¹³ But when you give a feast, invite the poor, the maimed, the lame, the blind.
¹⁴ And you will be blessed, because they cannot repay you; for you shall be repaid at the Resurrection of the just."

Jesus is teaching exactly what we have been learning, and that is the saints will receive their reward at the Resurrection.

DANIEL 12:13 (NKJV)

¹³ "But you, go your way till the end; for you shall rest, and will arise to your inheritance at the end of the days."

Here, Daniel is told by the heavenly messenger mentioned earlier in the chapter to go on his way until the end, because Daniel had been asking him about the end. Daniel is told he will rest, meaning he will die, and will arise in the Resurrection to his inheritance, which means he will receive his reward at the Resurrection. This gives even more clarification that the Resurrection of the saints is the time they will receive their reward. Even though Daniel is now in heaven, he will not receive his full inheritance and reward until the time of the Resurrection. The next passage of Scripture provides further understanding of this, and why.

HEBREWS 11:35-38 (NKJV)

³⁵ Women received their dead raised to life again. Others were tortured, not accepting deliverance, that they might obtain a better resurrection.
³⁶ Still others had trial of mocking's and scourging's, yes,

and of chains and imprisonment.

³⁷ They were stoned, they were sawn in two, were tempted, were slain with the sword. They wandered about in sheepskins and goatskins, being destitute, afflicted, tormented—

³⁸ of whom the world was not worthy. They wandered in deserts and mountains, in dens and caves of the earth.

Notice at the end of *verse 35*, it says, *"that they might obtain a better resurrection,"* revealing the Resurrection will be the time that they receive their reward for their suffering. These great saints not only knew the Resurrection was when they would receive their reward, they also knew that their suffering and sacrifice would give them a greater reward and inheritance at the Resurrection. One more important note on this passage, it says, *"women received their dead raised to life again,"* referring to an individual who has died and been brought back to life, and will die again, and then will be in either the Resurrection of Life or the Resurrection of Condemnation. Continuing the passage with *verses 39-40*.

HEBREWS 11:39-40 (NKJV)

³⁹ And all these, having obtained a good testimony through faith, did not receive the promise,

⁴⁰ God having provided something better for us, that they should not be made perfect apart from us.

So, this passage states it is God's intention that all be rewarded and made perfect together at the Resurrection, which explains why there is a Rapture and why it is part of the Resurrection; because everyone has to be there to receive their inheritance and be made perfect (receive their glorified bodies) together!

The answer to the question—Why are the living saints Raptured at the time of the Resurrection and the Lord's return? Because the Judgement and reward of all the saints together takes place at the Lord's Return and the Resurrection. This is where all the saints receive their reward and inheritance together, which means all the saints have to be there. Both those who have died and those still alive at the Lord's Return, and that is exactly what the second Rapture passage says in *1*

Corinthians 15:51-52.

I CORINTHIANS 15:51-52 (NKJV)

51 Behold, I tell you a mystery: We shall not all sleep, but we shall all be changed—
52 in a moment, in the twinkling of an eye, at the last trumpet. For the trumpet will sound, and the dead will be raised incorruptible, and we shall be changed.

We will not all sleep (we will not all die), but we will all be changed together at the Resurrection and Rapture. This was also an answer to the main question in a previous chapter; *Who is in the Rapture?* It helps us better understand why, because now we know why all the saints have to be in the Rapture and Resurrection together.

There is one more great event that follows soon after the Rapture that does not specifically answer the question of why, nor does it state all the saints have to be present, but it is such a significant event following the Lord's Return that it is not hard to understand why all the saints of all time will be present. The following passages describe this event.

REVELATION 19:7-9,11 (NKJV)

7 Let us be glad and rejoice and give Him glory, for the marriage of the Lamb has come, and His wife has made herself ready."
8 And to her it was granted to be arrayed in fine linen, clean and bright, for the fine linen is the righteous acts of the saints.
9 Then he said to me, "Write: 'Blessed are those who are called to the marriage supper of the Lamb!' " And he said to me, "These are the true sayings of God."
11 Now I saw heaven opened, and behold, a white horse. And He who sat on him was called Faithful and True, and in righteousness He judges and makes war.

This passage describes the Lord on a white horse coming for His bride, who has prepared herself for Him and the Marriage Supper of the Lamb. The Marriage Supper of the Lamb is the event I was referring to as the other very significant event that follows soon after the Rapture.

The next passage we will read describes the Marriage Supper of the Lamb.

MATTHEW 25:1-10 (NKJV)

¹ "Then the kingdom of heaven shall be likened to ten virgins who took their lamps and went out to meet the bridegroom.
² Now five of them were wise, and five were foolish.
³ Those who were foolish took their lamps and took no oil with them,
⁴ but the wise took oil in their vessels with their lamps.
⁵ But while the bridegroom was delayed, they all slumbered and slept.
⁶ "And at midnight a cry was heard: 'Behold, the bridegroom is coming; go out to meet him!'
⁷ Then all those virgins arose and trimmed their lamps.
⁸ And the foolish said to the wise, 'Give us some of your oil, for our lamps are going out.'
⁹ But the wise answered, saying, 'No, lest there should not be enough for us and you;
but go rather to those who sell, and buy for yourselves.'
¹⁰ And while they went to buy, the bridegroom came, and those who were ready went in with him to the wedding; and the door was shut.

This passage describes the bride (the Church) as ten virgins waiting for their bridegroom (Christ). Those who are ready are able to endure until the bridegroom comes, but the rest go back to trade with the world. When the Lord, the bridegroom, comes, those who are ready will go into the wedding and then the door will be shut. Both passages indicate a wedding is to take place soon after the Lord returns for His people. As I stated earlier, Scripture does not directly say that the Marriage Supper of the Lamb is why, at the Lord's return, the living saints have to be Raptured, but since we know all the saints are in the Resurrection and Rapture, and the fact that the Marriage Supper of the Lamb is a very significant event for God's people, I believe this gives us an even better understanding of why there is a Rapture of the saints that are still alive at the Lord's return. If there was only a Resurrection, the saints still alive at the Lord's return would miss this great event.

QUESTION 5

WHERE IS THE RAPTURE?

Let's see what Scripture says. We will start with the Rapture verses in *1 Thessalonians 4*.

1 THESSALONIANS 4:16-17 (NKJV)

16 For the Lord Himself will descend from heaven with a shout, with the voice of an
archangel, and with the trumpet of God. And the dead in Christ will rise first.
17 Then we who are alive and remain shall be caught up together with them in the
clouds to meet the Lord in the air. And thus we shall always be with the Lord.

The Scripture says the Lord descends from heaven to the clouds and we meet the Lord in the air, revealing that the Rapture is in the sky. Let's examine some other Scriptures about the Lord's return and see what else we can learn about where the Rapture takes place.

MARK 13:26 (NKJV)

26 Then they will see the Son of Man coming in the clouds with great power and glory.

Again, Scripture says *"in the clouds,"* but it also says something else important—they will see the Son of Man in the clouds. Who is they? Who will see Him? The next verse answers that question in *Revelation*.

REVELATION 1:7 (NKJV)

7 Behold, He is coming with clouds, and every eye will see Him, even they who pierced Him. And all the tribes of the earth will mourn because of Him. Even so, Amen.

It says every eye will see Him. So, the answer to the question—Who will see Him? Everyone will see Him. The whole world will witness the coming of Christ and the Rapture of those who truly belong to Him. Next, the verse says, *"And all the tribes of the earth will mourn."* The saints, if they mourn, will mourn for joy because they get to go and be with the Lord. Those who knew to be ready and are not ready will mourn because they are not prepared for His coming and will not get to go and be with the Lord. The unbelievers will mourn because they know that they have rejected Christ and will face judgment. There is one last aspect about where the Rapture will take place that I believe is important to know. We will look at that and then wrap this question up.

LUKE 17:24 (NKJV)

24 For as the lightning that flashes out of one part under heaven shines to the other part under heaven, so also the Son of Man will be in His day.

MATTHEW 24:27,29 (NKJV)

27 For as the lightning comes from the east and flashes to the west, so also will the coming of the Son of Man be.
29 the sun will be darkened, and the moon will not give its light; the stars will fall from heaven, and the powers of the heavens will be shaken.

The Lord is going to light up what will be very dark earth and sky when He comes, which is going to make Him visible to all. The answer to the question—*Where is the Rapture?* It is in the sky where everyone is going to see Him, and they will mourn when He comes.

QUESTION 6

HOW MANY RAPTURES ARE THERE?

Before we can answer this question, we need to review something we learned in the first chapter, and that is the word "Rapture" is not found in Scripture. It instead has become an acceptable word to use in place of the words *"caught up"* in the Rapture verse *1 Thessalonians 4:17*. Since the word Rapture is not in Scripture, we would not be able to find any other Raptures in Scripture using the word Rapture. So, the question is, are there any other Scriptures with the phrase *"caught up"*? The answer is yes. And to be thorough in our study, let's look at the passages of Scripture where these are found.

2 CORINTHIANS 12:2-4 (NKJV)

2 I know a man in Christ who fourteen years ago—whether in the body I do not know, or whether out of the body I do not know, God knows—such a one was caught up to the third heaven.

3 And I know such a man—whether in the body or out of the body I do not know, God knows—

4 how he was caught up into Paradise and heard inexpressible words, which it is not lawful for a man to utter.

In this passage of Scripture, Paul says he knows a man that was caught up to the third heaven, paradise, fourteen years before he wrote this epistle. He does not know whether he was in his body or if his spirit was caught up, and he heard inexpressible words not lawful for a man to utter. This is the Rapture of only one man who was caught up to paradise, not the sky where all the saints are gathered to Christ, and it also happened fourteen years before Paul wrote this epistle, making it clear this is not the Rapture of the Church at the coming of Christ and the Resurrection of the saints. The next place in Scripture that uses phrase *"caught up"* is in *Revelation 12*.

REVELATION 12:5 (NKJV)
5 She bore a male Child who was to rule all nations with a rod of iron. And her Child was caught up to God and His throne.

Who is the male Child caught up to God's throne? The next verse reveals who he is.

MARK 16:19 (NKJV)
19 So then, after the Lord had spoken to them, He was received up into heaven, and sat down at the right hand of God.

This verse shows Christ is the male Child who was caught up to heaven and sat down at the right-hand of God's throne. The next verse gives further proof that Jesus is the male Child that was caught up to God's throne.

REVELATION 19:15 (NKJV)
15 Now out of His mouth goes a sharp sword, that with it He should strike the nations. And He Himself will rule them with a rod of iron. He Himself treads the winepress of the fierceness and wrath of Almighty God.

This verse is describing Christ's return to the earth and shows it is Christ Himself who will rule the nations with a rod of iron, leaving no doubt who the male Child is in *Revelation 12:5*, a male Child who was to rule all nations with a rod of iron. That was the last passage of Scripture that has the phrase *"caught up"* in it. These two passages have four things that make them completely different from the passages of the Rapture of all the saints still alive at the coming of Christ and the Resurrection.

1. These are Raptures of individuals and not of all the saints still alive at the coming of Christ.
2. They are not at the coming of Christ.
3. These individuals are caught up to heaven and not the sky where all the saints are gathered to Christ at His coming.
4. There is no Resurrection at the time of these passages.

There are two more instances in Scripture where saints are caught up. The phrase *"caught up"* is not used, but a very similar phrase with the same meaning, and to be thorough in our study and make sure we do not overlook anything, let's look at these Scriptures as well. These are both in the book of Revelation, the first is in *Revelation 4*.

REVELATION 4:1 (NKJV)
¹ After these things I looked, and behold, a door standing open in heaven. And the first voice which I heard was like a trumpet speaking with me, saying, "Come up here, and I will show you things which must take place after this."

This verse is where the Apostle John is caught up to heaven and receives the visions that he writes, which become the book of *Revelation*. The Rapture of the Apostle John took place approximately two thousand years ago, like the previous Raptures we just studied.

1. It is the Rapture of an individual.
2. It is not at the coming of Christ.
3. The individual is caught up to heaven and not the sky.
4. These Raptures are not part of a Resurrection

The final passage where an individual is caught up, and in this case, there are actually two individuals caught up, is in *Revelation 11*.

REVELATION 11:3-12 (NKJV)
³ And I will give power to my two witnesses, and they will prophesy one thousand two hundred and sixty days, clothed in sackcloth."
⁴ These are the two olive trees and the two lampstands standing before the God of the earth.
⁵ And if anyone wants to harm them, fire proceeds from their mouth and devours their enemies. And if anyone

wants to harm them, he must be killed in this manner.

⁶ These have power to shut heaven, so that no rain falls in the days of their prophecy; and they have power over waters to turn them to blood, and to strike the earth with all plagues, as often as they desire.

⁷ When they finish their testimony, the beast that ascends out of the bottomless pit will make war against them, overcome them, and kill them.

⁸ And their dead bodies will lie in the street of the great city which spiritually is called Sodom and Egypt, where also our Lord was crucified.

⁹ Then those from the peoples, tribes, tongues, and nations will see their dead bodies three-and-a-half days, and not allow their dead bodies to be put into graves.

¹⁰ And those who dwell on the earth will rejoice over them, make merry, and send gifts to one another, because these two prophets tormented those who dwell on the earth.

¹¹ Now after the three-and-a-half days the breath of life from God entered them, and they stood on their feet, and great fear fell on those who saw them.

¹² And they heard a loud voice from heaven saying to them, "Come up here." And they ascended to heaven in a cloud, and their enemies saw them.

These passages describe the two witnesses, who are two great prophets during the time of the end that are killed after they finish their testimony. Then, after three-and-a-half days, the breath of life from God enters them and they rise to their feet and are commanded to come up to heaven and ascend to heaven in a cloud. Again, similar to the previous Raptures just examined—

1. It is the Rapture of two individuals.
2. It is not at the coming of Christ.
3. The individuals are caught up to heaven and not the sky.
4. There is a Resurrection of these two individuals, but not of all the saints.

There are two Raptures in the Old Testament of individuals taken to heaven while they were still alive on the earth, and they were Enoch

and Elijah. If we count all these Raptures, the answer to our question—*How many Raptures are there?* There are six Raptures. Except, five of these Raptures are of individuals who are caught up to heaven, not the Rapture of all the saints still alive at the Resurrection when the Lord comes in the sky, which is the real question we are trying to answer. So, changing our question; How many Raptures are there of the saints still alive at the Resurrection of the saints when Christ comes in the sky? There is only one Rapture. To be absolutely certain there is only one Rapture, we will study a key event that the Rapture is a part of, and that is the Resurrection of the saints.

JOHN 5:28-29 (NKJV)

28 Do not marvel at this; for the hour is coming in which all who are in the graves will hear His voice
29 and come forth—those who have done good, to the Resurrection of Life, and those who have done evil, to the Resurrection of Condemnation.

Jesus says all who are in the graves will be in one of two Resurrections, the Resurrection of Life for the righteous or the Resurrection of Condemnation for the wicked. That's only two Resurrections, and only one Resurrection for the righteous, which are those who are in Christ. Next, let's see what Paul says in *Acts 24*.

ACTS 24:15 (NKJV)

15 I have hope in God, which they themselves also accept, that there will be a Resurrection of the dead, both of the just and the unjust.

The Apostle Paul also states there are only two Resurrections. A Resurrection of the Just and a Resurrection of the Unjust. This agrees with what Jesus said, there are only two Resurrections, and as we just read, Jesus stated these Resurrections are for all who are in the graves, making these global Resurrections. One for all those in Christ and one for the ungodly who died without Christ. Let's read what the Prophet Daniel has to say about the Resurrections.

DANIEL 12:2 (NKJV)

2 And many of those who sleep in the dust of the earth shall awake,

some to everlasting life, Some to shame and everlasting contempt.

Daniel also says there are only two Resurrections. One to *"everlasting life"* and the other to *"shame and everlasting contempt."* All three of these witnesses say there are two Resurrections and only one Resurrection of the righteous. Scripture says a matter is settled on two or three witnesses, and there is one more witness, the Apostle John in the book of *Revelation*. The passage in the book of *Revelation* is a description of the actual Resurrection events and provides even more detail.

REVELATION 20:4-6 (NKJV)
4 And I saw thrones, and they sat on them, and judgment was committed to them. Then I saw the souls of those who had been beheaded for their witness to Jesus and for the word of God, who had not worshiped the beast or his image, and had not received his mark on their foreheads or on their hands. And they lived and reigned with Christ for a thousand years.
5 But the rest of the dead did not live again until the thousand years were finished. This is the first Resurrection.
6 Blessed and holy is he who has part in the first Resurrection. Over such the second death has no power, but they shall be priests of God and of Christ and shall reign with Him a thousand years.

Verse 6 says, *"Blessed and holy is he who has part in the first Resurrection. Over such the second death has no power."* The Scripture says this is the first Resurrection and blessed and holy are those who are part of this first Resurrection because the second death has no power over them. Jesus called the Resurrection of the *righteous "the Resurrection of Life."* We just learned from the Lord Jesus, the Apostle Paul, and the Prophet Daniel that there are only two Resurrections and only one Resurrection of the righteous, and they always spoke of the Resurrection of the righteous first and the Resurrection of the wicked second. It makes sense that the Resurrection of the righteous would be the first Resurrection, Jesus also said, *"all who are in the graves,"* that means everyone who has died, who belong to Christ, would be

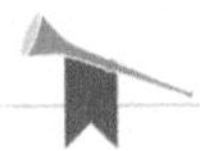

resurrected at this first Resurrection, making it a global Resurrection of all—everyone who is in Christ. This is exactly what the Rapture passages say, all who are in Christ will be in the Resurrection and Rapture at the Lord's coming.

I CORINTHIANS 15:51 (NKJV)
⁵¹ "Behold, I tell you a mystery: We shall not all sleep, but we shall all be changed."

I THESSALONIANS 4:16-17 (NKJV)
¹⁶ "and the dead in Christ will rise first.
¹⁷ Then we who are alive and remain shall be caught up together with them in the clouds to meet the Lord in the air."

Since this is the first and only global Resurrection of the saints, there cannot be another global Resurrection of all who are in Christ before this one. Leaving only one possible conclusion; The first Resurrection in *Revelation 20* and the Resurrection of the Rapture passages are the same Resurrection.

Continuing this passage, *verses 7-10* describe when the thousand years has ended and continues that description in *verses 11-15*, which includes the second Resurrection. We will pick up there and read about the second Resurrection.

REVELATION 20:11-15 (NKJV)
¹¹ Then I saw a great white throne and Him who sat on it, from whose face the earth and the heaven fled away. And there was found no place for them.
¹² And I saw the dead, small and great, standing before God, and books were opened. And another book was opened, which is the Book of Life. And the dead were judged according to their works, by the things which were written in the books.
¹³ The sea gave up the dead who were in it, and Death and Hades delivered up the dead who were in them. And they were judged, each one according to his works.
¹⁴ Then Death and Hades were cast into the lake of fire. This is the second death.

15 And anyone not found written in the Book of Life was cast into the lake of fire.

Here we see the Resurrection and judgment of unbelievers and they are cast into the lake of fire, which is the second death. This is the second and final Resurrection. There are no other Resurrections after this again, agreeing with what we have learned from our first three witnesses; The Lord Jesus, the Apostle Paul, and the Prophet Daniel, that there are only two Resurrections. One for the righteous, those in Christ, and one for the wicked, those not in Christ.

To make sure our examination of Scripture is thorough, I want to answer another question. Are there any other resurrections in Scripture that are not part of these two global Resurrections? Yes, there are, Jesus resurrected many people after they died, including the most notable one, the resurrection of Lazarus. Also, God, throughout some of the Old Testament prophets, resurrected individuals. But all of them would die again and will rise again in one of these two global Resurrections. And of course, there is the most important resurrection of all, the Resurrection of Christ Himself. At the time of Christ's Resurrection, there were some of the holy people who died in the past that came out of their graves immediately after Christ's Resurrection. Let's read those verses to see exactly what Scripture has to say.

MATTHEW 27:51-53 (NKJV)
51 Then, behold, the veil of the temple was torn in two from top to bottom; and the earth quaked, and the rocks were split,
52 and the graves were opened; and many bodies of the saints who had fallen asleep were raised;
53 and coming out of the graves after His Resurrection, they went into the holy city and appeared to many.

This passage says some of the saints who have fallen asleep (died) were raised and came out of the graves right after Christ's Resurrection who went into the city and appeared to many. This brings up the question of why these saints were resurrected at the time of Christ's Resurrection and did not have to wait for the global Resurrection of all the saints. *Verse 53* gives us one answer; *"they went into the holy city and appeared to many."* Though it does not say why they went into the holy city and appeared to many, the question is, why would God resurrect some of the saints from the past at the time of Christ's Resurrection and have them appear to many in the holy city? This what I believe, God chose some of the saints that had already died to be resurrected at the time of Christ's Resurrection to go into the holy city and appear to many because the Lord had just been crucified and resurrected, and many of His followers witnessed the horrible ordeal of His crucifixion and may not have known, or may be struggling to believe, that He had been resurrected and they would be in great sorrow. Therefore, the Lord chose some of the ancient saints to be resurrected when Christ was resurrected to go into the holy city and testify of Christ's Resurrection to comfort His followers who had just suffered witnessing the horrible crucifixion of their Lord. Christ's Resurrection is the *Resurrection of First Fruits* as revealed in *1 Corinthians 15:23.*

I CORINTHIANS 15:23 (NKJV)
²³ But each one in his own order: Christ the firstfruits, afterward those who are Christ's at His coming.

This verse clearly distinguishes Christ's Resurrection as the Resurrection of firstfruits from the Resurrection of the saints when He comes, which includes the Rapture of the saints still alive. The Resurrection when Christ comes is the first Resurrection, as revealed in *Revelation 20:4-6.* It is the first Resurrection of two global Resurrections, the Resurrection of those in Christ and the Resurrection of those not in Christ. In fact, the Resurrection of Christ, and those chosen to be resurrected with Him in the Resurrection of firstfruits, had already taken place before the Apostle Paul revealed the mystery of the Rapture that some of the saints will still be alive at the time of the Resurrection of the saints. Those still alive will be caught up (Raptured) in the air together to meet Christ at His coming. Now after a thorough examination of Scripture, we now know for certain how many Resurrections there are of those who are in Christ at His Coming, and that is, there is only one Resurrection of all those in Christ at His coming. And since the Rapture is part of the one and only Resurrection of those who belong to Christ when He comes, we now have with certainty the answer to the main question of this chapter.

How many Raptures are there? The answer is—one. There is only one Rapture of all those who are still alive and in Christ at the time of His coming and the Resurrection of Life.

To summarize what we learned in this chapter; Jesus said there are two Resurrections, the Resurrection of Life for the righteous and the Resurrection of Condemnation for the wicked. Paul said there are two Resurrections, the Resurrection of the Just and the Resurrection of the Unjust. Daniel's description of the Resurrections is the same, one Resurrection of Life for the righteous and one Resurrection of Condemnation for the wicked. *Revelation 20* reveals there is a first Resurrection for the righteous and a second and final Resurrection for the ungodly. The only other Resurrections aside from these two are the Resurrections of individuals who died and were resurrected to finish out their lives, and then die, and will be in one of the two global Resurrections. The Resurrection of Christ is the Resurrection of firstfruits and not the first global Resurrection, which is the Resurrection of all the saints that includes the Rapture. The Resurrection of firstfruits was before Paul ever wrote and revealed the mystery that the Rapture is part of the global Resurrection of the saints. Scripture is very clear, there are only two Resurrections of everyone in the graves, and only one Resurrection for all who are in the graves and in Christ. As we have learned from the Rapture passages in *1 Thessalonians 4:16-17* and *1 Corinthians 15:51-52*, the Rapture is part of the one and only Resurrection of those in the graves and in Christ, which gives us, with absolute certainty, the answer to our main question of this chapter. How many Raptures of all the saints left alive are there? The answer is—one.

A summary of the answers up to this point:

Is there a Rapture? Yes.

What is the Rapture? It is part of the Resurrection of the righteous. It is the catching up of the saints who are still alive and remain. It is an event at the coming of the Lord. It is a mystery revealed.

Who is in the Rapture? All the saints, living and dead when including the Resurrection.

Why is there a Rapture? It is the Judgement and Reward for all the saints together. For the Marriage Supper of the Lamb.

Where is the Rapture? In the sky where all eyes will see Christ at His coming.

How many Raptures are there? There is only one Rapture.

QUESTION 7

WHEN IS THE RAPTURE?

Now for the BIG Question! When is the Rapture? To understand what we can know about when the Rapture is, we will first look at what Jesus says about it.

MATTHEW 24:36 (NKJV)
36 "But of that day and hour no one knows, not even the angels of heaven, but My Father only.

MARK 13:29 (NKJV)
29 So you also, when you see these things happening, know that it is near—at the doors!

Jesus says we cannot know the day or hour. He was very specific when He said day or hour, which are very small measures of time, especially when compared with greater measures of time like years or months, or even a millennium. He did not, however, say that we could not know the year or month, or even the week. What Jesus did say is that we can know by the signs of things happening that the time is near. Therefore, the better we understand what Scripture says about the signs of the times, the better we will be able to interpret those signs and know that the time is near, even at the doors. With that said, let's see what Scripture can teach us about when the Rapture takes place. We have already learned from a previous question that the Rapture is part of the Resurrection, and since the Rapture immediately follows the Resurrection, if we learn from Scripture when the Resurrection takes place we will also know when the Rapture will happen. Let's continue to look at the Rapture passages for more answers to when the Rapture takes place.

I THESSALONIANS 4:16 (NKJV)

16 For the Lord Himself will descend from heaven with a shout, with the voice of an archangel, and with the trumpet of God. And the dead in Christ will rise first.

It says, *"with a shout, with the voice of an archangel, and with the trumpet of God."* Question—what is a Trumpet of God? For one, it would not be a trumpet of man. Since God dwells in heaven, the trumpet would come from heaven. God's servants in heaven are angels, so the trumpet would be sounded by an angel. The verse even says, *"with the voice of an archangel, and with the trumpet of God."* Confirming that the trumpet is coming from heaven and the angels. This is another answer to the question of when the Rapture is; it is at the Trumpet of God. Notice, this is not just any trumpet, it is *"the trumpet of God."* There is a trumpet mentioned in the other Rapture passage as well.

I CORINTHIANS 15:51-52 (NKJV)

51 Behold, I tell you a mystery: We shall not all sleep, but we shall all be changed—
52 in a moment, in the twinkling of an eye, at the last trumpet. For the trumpet will sound, and the dead will be raised incorruptible, and we shall be changed.

This passage not only says the Rapture is at the trumpet, but it also says which trumpet it is, and that is *"at the last trumpet."* Notice it does not say "a last trumpet," but "the last trumpet." Putting together what is revealed about the Rapture Trumpet from both Rapture passages, the Scriptures declare that the Rapture is at "the Last Trumpet of God," and since the Rapture trumpet is the Last Trumpet, it would be part of a series of Trumpets. As a series of trumpets, the earlier trumpets may have events that take place when they are sounded. These events could help us understand the signs of the times that Jesus spoke of, and therefore give us a better understanding of when the Rapture is going to take place. We will study these in detail in the second chapter of *"When is the Rapture?"*

There is one more answer to this question in these passages, and that is—the Rapture is at the coming of the Lord.

1 THESSALONIANS 4:15-17 (NKJV)

15 For this we say to you by the word of the Lord, that we who are alive and remain until the coming of the Lord will by no means precede those who are asleep.

16 For the Lord Himself will descend from heaven with a shout, with the voice of an archangel, and with the trumpet of God. And the dead in Christ will rise first.

17 Then we who are alive and remain shall be caught up together with them in the clouds to meet the Lord in the air. And thus we shall always be with the Lord.

To summarize these answers:

1. The Rapture is at the Resurrection.
2. The Rapture is at the Last Trumpet of God.
3. The Rapture is at the Coming of the Lord for His people.

Now that we have learned what the Rapture passages have to teach us about when the Rapture is, let's take those answers and thoroughly examine what Scripture has to say about them in order to gain a better understanding on timing of the Rapture. We will start with the first answer; the Rapture is part of the Resurrection. We have studied several passages concerning the Resurrection, and one very important fact we have learned is that there are only two global Resurrections; One for the saints and all those who have died in Christ, and one for the ungodly and all those who have died in their sins without Christ. Let's take a closer look in *Revelation 20* at the first Resurrection, the Resurrection of the saints.

REVELATION 20:4-6 (NKJV)

4 And I saw thrones, and they sat on them, and judgment was committed to them. Then I saw the souls of those who had been beheaded for their witness to Jesus and for the word of God, who had not worshiped the beast or his image, and had not received his mark on their foreheads or on their hands. And they lived and reigned with Christ for a thousand years.

5 But the rest of the dead did not live again until the thousand years were finished. This

is the first Resurrection.
⁶ Blessed and holy is he who has part in the first Resurrection. Over such the second death has no power, but they shall be priests of God and of Christ, and shall reign with Him a thousand years.

The passage says there are souls who are beheaded (martyred) for their witness to Jesus and for the word of God. This gives what I believe is special recognition to those who have died for Christ. It goes on to say that they did not worship the beast or his image and did not receive his mark on their foreheads or hands. Question—Who is this beast, and what is his image they did not worship and his mark they did not receive on their foreheads or hands? One important fact we can take from this passage is that the first Resurrection is after the time of this beast, his image, and his mark. So, learning who this beast is, and when his time is, will help us better understand when the Resurrection and Rapture will take place. Before we investigate who this beast is, let's look at the second answer we learned from the Rapture passages about when the Rapture takes place; The Rapture is at the Last Trumpet of God. To start with, we will read the Rapture verses to answer one more question—What is the Last Trumpet of God?

1 CORINTHIANS 15:52 (NKJV)
⁵² in a moment, in the twinkling of an eye, at the last trumpet. For the trumpet will sound, and the dead will be raised incorruptible, and we shall be changed.

1 THESSALONIANS 4:16 (NKJV)
¹⁶ For the Lord Himself will descend from heaven with a shout, with the voice of an archangel, and with the trumpet of God. And the dead in Christ will rise first.

Now that we have read those verses again, let's review the answer to the question—What is the Last Trumpet of God?

1. It is not a trumpet of man, or from the earth.
2. Since God is in heaven, it would be sounded from heaven.
3. God's servants in heaven are angels, so it would be sounded by an angel.
4. It would be the Last Trumpet sounded in heaven by angels.

There is a series of Trumpets of God sounded by angels in the book of *Revelation*, the last book of the Bible, and the Last Trumpet in this series would be the very Last Trumpet of God and the very Last Trumpet in Scripture. First, we will look at where these Trumpets begin to help us gain a better understanding of what these Trumpets are, this is found in *Revelation 8*.

REVELATION 8:1-2,6 (NKJV)
[1] When He opened the Seventh Seal, there was silence in heaven for about half an hour.
[2] And I saw the seven angels who stand before God, and to them were given seven trumpets.
[6] So the seven angels who had the seven trumpets prepared themselves to sound.

These verses let us know that there are Seven Trumpets, so we know the Last Trumpet will be the Seventh Trumpet. Let's go to the Seventh Trumpet found in *Revelation 11:15-18*.

REVELATION 11:15 (NKJV)
[15] Then the seventh angel sounded: And there were loud voices in heaven, saying, "The kingdoms of this world have become the kingdoms of our Lord and of His Christ, and He shall reign forever and ever!"

The sounding of the Seventh Trumpet is declaring the kingdoms of the world now belong to God and Christ, which is a clear indication that the Lord is coming soon to take back what belongs to Him. The next three verses are heaven worshiping the Lord. *Verse 18* continues with what is going to happen next.

REVELATION 11:18 (NKJV)
[18] The nations were angry, and Your wrath has come, And the time of the dead, that they should be judged, And that You should reward Your servants the prophets and the saints, And those who fear Your name, small and great, And should destroy those who destroy the earth."

This is the Resurrection because it is the judgment of the dead. It makes clear what group of the dead it is because it says it is time to reward His servants, prophets, and saints. We learned in chapter four, the Resurrection and Rapture of the righteous is a blessed ceremony where all the saints will receive their inheritance and rewards together. So, this Seventh Trumpet in *Revelation* is The Last Trumpet of God and the Resurrection of the saints, which makes perfect sense because the Rapture is at The Last Trumpet of God and the Resurrection of the saints.

The list of answers to when the Rapture is, according to the Seventh Trumpet in the book of *Revelation*, is shown below. These are the exact same answers as the Rapture passages provided, leaving no doubt, the Seventh Trumpet of God in the book of *Revelation* is the Last Trumpet of God in the Rapture passages. And since there is only one Resurrection and Rapture of all who are in Christ, the Seventh Trumpet is the Resurrection and Rapture the saints.

1.   The Seventh Trumpet is the Resurrection.
2.   The Seventh Trumpet is the Last Trumpet of God.
3.   The Seventh Trumpet is sounded at the return of the Lord.

The Seventh Trumpet is the actual sounding of a Trumpet and not just a reference to it, the other Six Trumpets that proceed it are also the actual sounding of Trumpets. All Seven Trumpets have events that occur when each are sounded, we can study the events of the first Six Trumpets to help us understand the signs of the times that Jesus taught us to watch for, and therefore help us understand when the Rapture is going to happen. Before we look at any of the first Six Trumpets, let's investigate who this terrible beast character is that the saints who overcame and did not worship him or his image, or take his mark, were given special recognition and honor in the first Resurrection. Since the Resurrection of the saints is at the Seventh Trumpet, and the time of the beast is before that, we should be able to find this beast somewhere in the previous Trumpets. He is first mentioned in the time of the Sixth Trumpet.

REVELATION 9:13 (NKJV)
13 Then the sixth angel sounded: And I heard a voice from the four horns of the golden altar which is before God,

The Sixth Trumpet is sounded and continues through the rest of *Revelation 9*, then continues again in *Revelation 11* and ends at *Revelation 11:13*. We are not going to cover everything on the Sixth Trumpet at this point, we will do that later, we will focus on this beast character right now. He is first mentioned in *Revelation 11:7*, so we will start with *Revelation 11:1* to understand what this chapter reveals about this beast. The book of *Revelation* has a lot more to say about the beast, but this is where it begins. We need to start at the beginning so we can understand the time when the beast will be on the earth.

REVELATION 11:1-3 (NKJV)

¹ Then I was given a reed like a measuring rod. And the angel stood, saying, "Rise and measure the temple of God, the altar, and those who worship there.
² But leave out the court which is outside the temple, and do not measure it, for it has been given to the Gentiles. And they will tread the holy city underfoot for forty-two months.
³ And I will give power to my two witnesses, and they will prophesy one thousand two hundred and sixty days, clothed in sackcloth."

Verse 3 says *"And I will give power to my two witnesses."* The word "And" in this verse indicates that this is an inclusion not a continuation, meaning the gentiles trampling the holy city and the two witnesses prophesying occur at the same time. It says the gentiles will trample the holy city for *forty-two months* and the two witnesses will prophecy *one-thousand-two-hundred-and-sixty days*. Forty-two months and one-thousand-two-hundred-and-sixty days are equal measures of time, so the gentiles trampling the holy city and the two witnesses prophesying occur at the same time and for the same length of time. Why give the same length of time in two different ways? One reason, it would help the reader understand it really is forty-two months, and equally, one-thousand-two-hundred-and-sixty days, and not to try and interpret these as different measures of time. It accomplishes this because you can't change the number of days or months to some other measure of time and still be equal. The actual words used in the Greek are translated days for days and months for months as stated in the English text. Why does God reveal the length of time? The first obvious reason is that God wants us to know, otherwise it would not be in Scripture. But why does He want us to know? I believe it is because these are terrible times and God wants us to know how long it will last so we can prepare ourselves to be able to endure them. *Verses 4-6* describe the testimony of the two witnesses and *verse 7* is where the beast comes in. We will look at that next.

REVELATION 11:7 (NKJV)
7 When they finish their testimony, the beast that ascends out of the bottomless pit will make war against them, overcome them, and kill them.

We see that this beast is the one who kills the two witnesses, which means this beast is present during the time of the Sixth Trumpet. This beast must be a powerful character to be able to kill the two witnesses, because, until the beast kills them, no one is able to kill them. *Revelation 11:5* says the two witnesses are able bring fire down on their enemies and kill them. Now that we know this beast is present during the Sixth Trumpet, let's learn who this beast character really is and how he operates.

REVELATION 13:1-2 (NKJV)
1 Then I stood on the sand of the sea. And I saw a beast rising up out of the sea, having seven heads and ten horns, and on his horns ten crowns, and on his heads a blasphemous name.
2 Now the beast which I saw was like a leopard, his feet were like the feet of a bear, and his mouth like the mouth of a lion. The dragon gave him his power, his throne, and great authority.

The seven heads and ten horns represent kings and kingdoms, and *Revelation 17* gives more detail on these. The book of *Daniel* gives a detailed description of the bear, lion, and leopard. For now, understand that these also represent kings and kingdoms. We'll be covering these in detail later. It says the dragon gave the beast his power, his throne, and great authority. To understand who empowers this beast, let's look and see who this dragon is that gives him his power, his throne, and great authority. *Revelation 12* reveals who this dragon is.

REVELATION 12:3 (NKJV)

³ And another sign appeared in heaven: behold, a great, fiery red dragon having seven heads and ten horns, and seven diadems on his heads.

Notice this dragon has seven heads and ten horns like the beast, except the beast has crowns on the ten horns and the dragon has crowns on the seven heads. The word "diadems" used in this verse means "crowns." The heads and horns represent kings and kingdoms just like they do on the beast. Now let's see who this dragon really is in *verse 9.*

REVELATION 12:9,12 (NKJV)

⁹ So the great dragon was cast out, that serpent of old, called the Devil and Satan, who deceives the whole world; he was cast to the earth, and his angels were cast out with him.
¹² Therefore rejoice, O heavens, and you who dwell in them! Woe to the inhabitants of the earth and the sea! For the devil has come down to you, having great wrath, because he knows that he has a short time."

The dragon is the Devil and Satan. He has just been cast down to the earth having great wrath, in other words, he has been cast down to the earth and is full of rage because he knows his time is almost over. Satan has been ruling the earth from the second heaven, which is the space between the first heaven and the third heaven, which is between the earth's sky and God's throne. Near the end of the age, Satan, and his angels (demons), will be cast down to the earth. The verse says, *"Woe to inhabitants of the earth and sea! For the devil has come down to you. Having great wrath, because he knows that he has a short time."* Not only is the devil himself empowering this beast, but the devil who has been cast down and is now trapped on the earth, running out of time and full of rage. Woe is right, the last three of the Seven Trumpets of God are also called "Woes," and we will learn about them later. The difference is that this woe is describing the wrath of Satan, and the Seven Trumpets are the Judgements of God. Now we know who is empowering this beast, let's continue learning who the beast really is.

REVELATION 13:3-4 (NKJV)

3 And I saw one of his heads as if it had been mortally wounded, and his deadly wound was healed. And all the world marveled and followed the beast.
4 So they worshiped the dragon who gave authority to the beast; and they worshiped the beast, saying, "Who is like the beast? Who is able to make war with him?"

The entire world is in awe and wonder and follow the beast. They even worship the beast declaring *"Who is able to make war with him?"* after he was healed from a mortal wound. This would indicate he was a great conqueror, and through war, became mortally wounded and was heal by the power of Satan. Why a mortal wound and being healed from near death instead of a true death and resurrection like Jesus Christ? Because this is a counterfeit of the Resurrection of Christ. And Satan, not being God, cannot resurrect anyone. God has reserved the power of true resurrection for Himself alone! Why is this important? To help God's people to not be fooled by this counterfeit resurrection of the beast, who is the antichrist. But to a deceived world who has already rejected the True and Living God and His far greater power, they are going to worship this antichrist because of this counterfeit resurrection.

REVELATION 13:5 (NKJV)

5 And he was given a mouth speaking great things and blasphemies, and he was given authority to continue for forty-two months.

Forty-two months, that's the same measure of time during the Sixth Trumpet that the gentiles trample the outer courts of the temple and the two witness's testimony of one-thousand-two-hundred-and-sixty days, which is also forty-two months. The beast kills them near the end of the Sixth Trumpet, which is the second woe.

REVELATION 11:7,14 (NKJV)

7 When they finish their testimony, the beast that ascends out of the bottomless pit will make war against them, overcome them, and kill them.
14 The second woe is past. Behold, the third woe is coming quickly.

At the Seventh Trumpet, it is announced that the world and its kingdoms have become the Lord's, declaring the beginning of Christ's reign and the beginning of the end of the reign of the beast.

REVELATION 11:15 (NKJV)

15 Then the seventh angel sounded: And there were loud voices in heaven, saying, "The kingdoms of this world have become the kingdoms of our Lord and of His Christ, and He shall reign forever and ever!"

The beast's forty-two-month reign ends some time very soon after the Seventh Trumpet, and we know the Sixth Trumpet is at least forty-two months long because the gentiles trampling the outer courts and the two witnesses prophesying are one-thousand-two-hundred-and-sixty days. This means the forty-two months of ruling authority granted to the beast has to start sometime during the Sixth Trumpet, with most of it during the time of the Sixth Trumpet. This beast did not just come on the scene at the Sixth Trumpet, remember, he is being worshiped for being mortally wounded and miraculously healed by the power of Satan. The people praise him saying *"Who can make war with the beast."* This means he was already a great conqueror who suffered a mortal wound in battle and was healed by the power of Satan. As we will read next, the beast is now a global ruler after receiving his power and authority from the dragon.

REVELATION 13:6-8 (NKJV)

6 Then he opened his mouth in blasphemy against God, to blaspheme His name, His tabernacle, and those who dwell in heaven.
7 It was granted to him to make war with the saints and to overcome them. And authority was given him over every tribe, tongue, and nation.
8 All who dwell on the earth will worship him, whose names have not been written in the Book of Life of the Lamb slain from the foundation of the world.

This evil beast, the antichrist, really thinks he is God, demanding everyone in the world to worship him, and everyone not written in the book of life will worship him. With great malice, he slanders God, His name, tabernacle, and everyone in heaven. This beast now has global

authority and is making war with the saints, and since he is a ruler with authority over all the nations, it means all the nations are going to be at war with the saints.

REVELATION 13:11-14 (NKJV)

11 Then I saw another beast coming up out of the earth, and he had two horns like a lamb and spoke like a dragon.
12 And he exercises all the authority of the first beast in his presence and causes the earth and those who dwell in it to worship the first beast, whose deadly wound was healed.
13 He performs great signs, so that he even makes fire come down from heaven on the earth in the sight of men.
14 And he deceives those who dwell on the earth by those signs which he was granted to do in the sight of the beast,

This second beast is also known as the "false prophet," found in *Revelation 16:13, 19:20* and *20:10.* This false prophet is forcing the whole earth to worship this first beast—the antichrist. He's performing counterfeit operations of the Holy Spirit, who was sent to lead people to Christ. Notice it says, *"he performs great signs."* This is a deliberate public performance of satanic power to create a worldwide deception so all people will fear and worship the beast. Also note, this passage says three separate times that the world will worship the beast.

REVELATION 13:14-15 (NKJV)

14 And he deceives those who dwell on the earth by those signs which he was granted to do in the sight of the beast, telling those who dwell on the earth to make an image to the beast who was wounded by the sword and lived.
15 He was granted power to give breath to the image of the beast, that the image of the beast should both speak and cause as many as would not worship the image of the beast to be killed.

There is coming a time during the reign of the beast that the whole world is not only going to be commanded to worship the beast, but they are going to be forced to worship his image or be killed. This image of the beast will be a statue of the beast, and through satanic power it will appear to be alive because it will be breathing and speaking. It is not hard to figure out who will not worship this image of

the beast, which is an idol. This will be the worst persecution of God's holy people ever because they will have to choose between worshiping an idol, the image of the beast, or be put to death in a world where most people will be following and worshiping this beast and his image, and for their own survival, and perhaps the potential favor they might gain with this evil empire, they will turn in anyone and everyone that does not worship the image of the beast.

REVELATION 13:16-18 (NKJV)
[16] He causes all, both small and great, rich and poor, free and slave, to receive a mark on their right hand or on their foreheads,
[17] and that no one may buy or sell except one who has the mark or the name of the beast, or the number of his name.
[18] Here is wisdom. Let him who has understanding calculate the number of the beast, for it is the number of a man: His number is 666.

There is not only worldwide pressure and persecution to worship the beast, and eventually his image, but the saints will not be able to buy or sell anything, including the most basic needs like food, water, and clothing. This mark is a replacement for money. Jesus taught that you cannot serve God and mammon, which is money and material wealth. You will either love one and hate the other, you cannot serve both, *Matthew 6:24*. When times are easy, it is easy to serve both because you are not forced to make a choice, but these will be the worst of times and what people truly love and trust will come to the surface. This is a clear warning from Jesus. Jesus fed the five thousand with five loaves and two fish, and the four thousand with seven loaves and few little fish, *Matthew 14:17-21 and Matthew 15:34-38*. God's people are going to have to completely rely on Him for everything. If you remember in the first Resurrection, special honor was given to those who did not worship the beast and his image or take his mark. Now let's see what happens to those who do.

REVELATION 14:9-11 (NKJV)
[9] Then a third angel followed them, saying with a loud voice, "If anyone worships the beast and his image, and receives his mark on his forehead or on his hand,
[10] he himself shall also drink of the wine of the wrath of

God, which is poured out full strength into the cup of His indignation. He shall be tormented with fire and brimstone in the presence of the holy angels and in the presence of the Lamb.

[11] And the smoke of their torment ascends forever and ever; and they have no rest day or night, who worship the beast and his image, and whoever receives the mark of his name."

You do not get a more serious warning than this. Those who worship the beast and his image or take his mark will suffer eternal punishment of fire and brimstone forever. Let's look at other Scripture witnesses that confirm everything we have just learned. Before we do that, because we have covered a lot of ground, I want to summarize everything we have learned about when the Rapture takes place.

1.   The Rapture is part of the Resurrection, which is the first of two Resurrections and the only Resurrection of the saints.
2.   The Rapture is at the Last Trumpet, which is the Seventh and Last Trumpet in the book of Revelation and the entire Bible.
3.   The Rapture is at the coming of the Lord for His people.
4.   The Rapture is after the forty-two-month global rein of the beast-antichrist, which occurs during the Sixth Trumpet of the book of Revelation, which is also confirmed by the descriptions in the First Resurrection of the saints who overcome the beast, his image, and his mark.

In earlier chapters, we learned the Apostle Paul wrote letters to the Thessalonians and Corinthians introducing the Rapture to them. Those letters are the Rapture passages that we have been studying. Now we are going to look at a second letter Paul writes to the Thessalonians about the Rapture.

2 THESSALONIANS 2:1-2 (NKJV)
[1] Now, brethren, concerning the coming of our Lord Jesus Christ and our gathering together to Him, we ask you,
[2] not to be soon shaken in mind or troubled, either by spirit or by word or by letter, as if from us, as though the day of Christ had come.

In this second letter, he is addressing their fears and concerns that the Rapture had already taken place. Let's see what he says to them about that.

2 THESSALONIANS 2:3 (NKJV)
3 Let no one deceive you by any means; for that Day will not come unless the falling away comes first, and the man of sin is revealed, the son of perdition

The Apostle Paul gives them an urgent warning saying, *"Let no one deceive you by means."* The day of Christ and our gathering together to Him will not happen until after the falling away and the man of sin is revealed. Who is this man of sin, the son of perdition, which means hell? The next few verses give more detail on who this man of sin is and how he is revealed.

2 THESSALONIANS 2:4,9-10 (NKJV)
4 who opposes and exalts himself above all that is called God or that is worshiped, so that he sits as God in the temple of God, showing himself that he is God.
9 The coming of the lawless one is according to the working of Satan, with all power, signs, and lying wonders,
10 and with all unrighteous deception among those who perish, because they did not receive the love of the truth, that they might be saved.

Scripture says this man of sin, who is the son of perdition and the lawless one, sits in God's temple, claiming to be God and opposes God, and exalts himself above God and the worship of God. By the power and works of Satan he performs signs and wonders and deceives everyone who does not receive the love of the truth. That's exactly what the beast and his false prophet do in the book of *Revelation*. Compare the man of sin to the beast in *Revelation 13*.

REVELATION 13:5,8,13-14 (NKJV)
5 And he was given a mouth speaking great things and blasphemies, and he was given authority to continue for forty-two months.
8 All who dwell on the earth will worship him, whose names have not been written in the Book of Life of the

Lamb slain from the foundation of the world.
¹³ He performs great signs, so that he even makes fire come down from heaven on the earth in the sight of men.
¹⁴ And he deceives those who dwell on the earth by those signs which he was granted to do in the sight of the beast,

These Scriptures leave little to no doubt who this man of sin is. But the next Scripture leaves no doubt who he is.

2 THESSALONIANS 2:8 (NKJV)

⁸ And then the lawless one will be revealed, whom the Lord will consume with the breath of His mouth and destroy with the brightness of His coming.

This verse says the Lord is going to destroy the lawless one, who is the man of sin, at His coming. Comparing this to what the book of *Revelation* says about the beast when the Lord returns to the earth.

REVELATION 19:11, 19-21 (NKJV)

¹¹ Now I saw heaven opened, and behold, a white horse. And He who sat on him was called Faithful and True, and in righteousness He judges and makes war.
¹⁹ And I saw the beast, the kings of the earth, and their armies, gathered together to make war against Him who sat on the horse and against His army.
²⁰ Then the beast was captured, and with him the false prophet who worked signs in his presence, by which he deceived those who received the mark of the beast and those who worshiped his image. These two were cast alive into the lake of fire burning with brimstone.
²¹ And the rest were killed with the sword which proceeded from the mouth of Him who sat on the horse.

Scripture is very clear, leaving no doubt who the man the sin, the son of perdition, is. He is the beast in the book of *Revelation*, the antichrist, who Christ will destroy we He returns to the earth. Now that we know for certain who the man of sin is, let's review what Paul was saying to the Thessalonians about the timing of the Rapture in relation to the revelation of the man if sin.

2 THESSALONIANS 2:1-3 (NKJV)
[1] Now, brethren, concerning the coming of our Lord Jesus Christ and our gathering together to Him, we ask you,
[2] not to be soon shaken in mind or troubled, either by spirit or by word or by letter, as if from us, as though the day of Christ had come.
[3] Let no one deceive you by any means; for that Day will not come unless the falling away comes first, and the man of sin is revealed, the son of perdition,

The Apostle Paul is clearly saying *"the coming of our Lord Jesus Christ and our gathering together to Him,"* which is the Rapture, will not happened until after the man of sin is revealed. We have learned how he is revealed, and with that understanding, we know with absolute certainty that he is the beast in the book of *Revelation*. Comparing this to what the Apostle John wrote in the book of *Revelation* about the first Resurrection, which is the one and only global Resurrection of the saints that includes the Rapture, it is after the coming of the beast. There is complete agreement between what the Apostle Paul wrote in his second letter to the Thessalonians and what the Apostle John wrote in the book of *Revelation*. The Resurrection and Rapture happen after the coming of the beast. There is one more thing the Apostle Paul says that must happen before the Rapture.

2 THESSALONIANS 2:3 (NKJV)
[3] Let no one deceive you by any means; for that Day will not come unless the falling away comes first, and the man of sin is revealed, the son of perdition.

The falling away must come first. In the Apostles Paul's fourth letter to Timothy, he describes the falling away.

1 TIMOTHY 4:1 (NKJV)
[1] Now the Spirit expressly says that in latter times some will depart from the faith, giving heed to deceiving spirits and doctrines of demons

Paul says the falling away will happen in the last days and that some believers will depart from the faith, instead, they will believe the doctrines of demons taught to them by deceiving spirits. With this being the last days, and the Gospel having been preached to the whole world, the falling away will be on a global scale, and Paul said the falling away was first, before the man of sin, the antichrist. Since these fallen believers will already be following demons, they will naturally follow the antichrist, and nonbelievers already follow demons so following the antichrist is most definitely going to be normal for them. A global falling away of believers is a definite sign we are in the last days. The parable of the ten virgins in *Matthew 25* is another passage of Scripture that reveals the falling away.

There is one more thing Paul wrote in his second letter to the Thessalonians that is related to the Rapture that we should look at before we look at our third witness.

2 THESSALONIANS 2:6-8 (NKJV)
[6] And now you know what is restraining, that he may be revealed in his own time.
[7] For the mystery of lawlessness is already at work; only He who now restrains will do so until He is taken out of the way.
[8] And then the lawless one will be revealed,

It says that lawlessness is already at work and is being restrained by someone. It does not say who that someone is, though many believe it is the Holy Spirit, and that is likely true since He is God and has the power to restrain evil on global scale. The Holy Spirit is also in charge of all the holy angels, including Michael and his army, and it is also possible the holy angels may be assisting the Holy Spirit in holding back the evil. But it says he is taken out of the way so the lawless one can be revealed. We know from what we have learned from the book of *Revelation* and Paul's second letter to the Thessalonians that the antichrist comes before the Resurrection and Rapture. So, what does it mean for the Holy Spirit to be taken out of the way? Since God's true holy people, the saints, have the Holy Spirit and will still be here during the time of the beast, I believe the Holy Spirit has not left God's people but has done exactly what the Scripture says; He has been taken away from a world full of people who have rejected Christ and is no longer restraining the evil so the lawless one can be revealed. The Holy Spirit will still be with all true believers. Believers could not endure to the end

without the Holy Spirit. In fact, the parable of the ten virgins in *Matthew 25* shows that those who don't have enough oil in their lamps do not endure to the end. This oil is a representation of the Holy Spirit.

Now that we have examined both the book of Revelation and what Paul wrote in his second letter to the Thessalonians about the Rapture, and that Scripture reveals that the Rapture is after the coming of the antichrist and the great persecution against the saints, there is one more witness to examine and He gets the Final Word.

To summarize up to this point; the Apostle Paul said the Rapture cannot happen until after the man of sin, the beast, who is the antichrist, comes. This is in full agreement with what the Apostle John wrote in the book *Revelation*. Paul said the falling away of believers on a global scale will also happen before the Rapture and would also precede the coming of the antichrist. The Apostle Paul also said the one holding back the evil would be taken away from the world, and it is believed this person is the Holy Spirit. True believers will still have the Holy Spirit, but He would no longer be holding back the evil from the world. With God no longer holding back the evil, and the evil one, the antichrist, ruling all the nations, the world is going to be a very evil place, and for true Christians, it is going to be a very hostile world. In fact, in *Revelation 13*, it says the beast will be in an all-out war with the saints.

REVELATION 13:7 (NKJV)
7 It was granted to him to make war with the saints and to overcome them. And authority was given him over every tribe, tongue, and nation.

THE FINAL WORD

Jesus taught about the Rapture and the timing of when the Rapture would take place, and since He is the Word of God, no one deserves the final word more than Him. Let's read what Jesus has to say about when the Rapture is.

MARK 13:26-27 (NKJV)
26 Then they will see the Son of Man coming in the clouds with great power and glory.
27 And then He will send His angels, and gather together His elect from the four winds, from the farthest part of earth to the farthest part of heaven.

MATTHEW 24:31 (NKJV)
31 And He will send His angels with a great sound of a trumpet, and they will gather together His elect from the four winds, from one end of heaven to the other.

Jesus gives us three answers to the question of when the Rapture is from these verses.

WHEN IS THE RAPTURE?

It is at the coming of the Lord.
26 Then they will see the Son of Man coming in the clouds with great power and glory.

It is at the Resurrection.

²⁷ And then He will send His angels, and gather together His elect from the four winds, from the farthest part of earth to the farthest part of heaven.

This verse contains the Rapture and the Resurrection; *"from the farthest part of earth"* is the Rapture and *"the farthest part of heaven"* is the Resurrection.

It is at the trumpet of God.
³¹ And He will send His angels with a great sound of a trumpet, and they will gather together His elect from the four winds, from one end of heaven to the other.

Since the Lord Himself is initiating this trumpet, and its coming from heaven and an angel, we know this is a trumpet of God and not a trumpet of man. These are the exact same answer to a question from a previous chapter that came from the Rapture passages. Let's see if these verses give us the same answers for the rest of our questions from the Rapture passages. We will go back to the first question and answer all the questions in the same order as we did with the Rapture passages.

IS THERE A RAPTURE?

Since we have already established there is a Rapture, the real question is—is the Rapture in these verses? The Rapture and Resurrection are both in *verse 27*.

MATTHEW 13:27 (NKJV)
²⁷ "And then He will send His angels, and gather together His elect from the four winds, from the farthest part of earth to the farthest part of heaven."

Those gathered from the farthest part of the earth is the Rapture of the saints left alive at the coming of the Lord, and those gathered from the farthest part of heaven are the saints who have died and come with the Lord and are resurrected at His coming in the sky.

Is the Rapture in these verses? Yes

WHAT IS THE RAPTURE?

It is the coming of the Lord for his people and the Resurrection of the saints.

> 26 Then they will see the Son of Man coming in the clouds with great power and glory.

The Lord is gathering His people from *"the farthest part of earth,"* which is the catching up of the saints still alive on the earth. In other words, the Rapture. The Lord is also gathering His people from *"the farthest part of heaven,"* the saints coming with the Lord from heaven will be in Resurrection. Again, these are the same answers that came from the Rapture passages.

WHO IS IN THE RAPTURE?

All of God's people. Everyone in Christ.

> 27 "And then He will send His angels, and gather together His elect from the four winds, from the farthest part of earth to the farthest part of heaven."

Verse 27 does not just say those in heaven or those on the earth, it says, *"the farthest part of earth"* and *"the farthest part of heaven."* Meaning to the very ends of the earth and to the very ends of heaven, which is all of heaven and all of earth, and that means all the saints in both heaven and earth are gathered to the Lord at His Coming.

WHY IS THERE A RAPTURE?

Because of the Judgement seat of Christ where everyone in Christ must be there together to receive their judgement and reward together, and for the saints still alive on the earth at the time of the Resurrection.

The answer in these *verses* is the same as the Rapture passages, and that answer is; Because there are saints still alive on the earth when the Lord comes. The rest of the answers to why there is a Rapture comes from what we learned in the Resurrection Scriptures and other passages of Scripture, and that is because the judgement seat of Christ is at the Resurrection and all the saints, the whole body of Christ, must be there because we will all receive our judgement and reward together, and that is followed by another very important event—the Marriage Supper of the Lamb.

HOW MANY RAPTURES ARE THERE?

Jesus only taught about gathering all His people to Himself. Only one time it is recorded in three of the four Gospels, *Matthew*, *Mark*, and *Luke*, but it is the same teaching in all three Gospels. Just like when we answered this question the first time to be sure there is only one Rapture, finding that the Rapture is part of the Resurrection, we studied the teachings in Scripture on the Resurrection and learned from them that there is only one Resurrection of all the saints. And since the Rapture is part of that Resurrection, there can only be one Rapture of the saints. There is only one Rapture of the saints!

WHERE IS THE RAPTURE?

In the clouds. In the sky.

²⁶ Then they will see the Son of Man coming in the clouds with great power and glory.

A list of answers about the Rapture from Jesus in the Gospels and the Apostle Paul in his epistles:

QUESTION	PAUL'S ANSWER	JESUS' ANSWER
Is There a Rapture?	*Yes.*	*Yes.*
What is the Rapture?	*The coming of the Lord, included in the Resurrection of the saints.*	*The coming of the Lord, included in the Resurrection of the saints.*
Who is in the Rapture?	*All the saints still alive on the earth at the coming of the Lord.*	*All the saints still alive on the earth at the coming of the Lord.*
Why is there a Rapture?	*Because of the Judgement seat of Christ.*	*Because of the Judgement seat of Christ.*
Where is the Rapture?	*In the Sky.*	*In the Sky.*
How many Raptures?	*One.*	*One.*
When is the Rapture?	*At the coming of the Lord, the Resurrection, and the Last Trumpet of God.*	*At the coming of the Lord, the Resurrection, and the Trumpet of God.*

We have examined the teachings of our Lord Jesus Christ on the Rapture and compared them to the teachings of the Apostle Paul's Rapture passages using the same complete set of questions and got the same answers. This should remove any doubt, if there was any, that Jesus and Paul are teaching about the same thing here, and that is the one and only global Rapture and Resurrection of the Church. Now, continuing our original question of this chapter—*When is the Rapture?* Before we continue and learn more of what the Lord has to say about when the Rapture takes place, I'm going to address one more thing so that there is absolutely no doubt Jesus is teaching about the Rapture. There are two words that Jesus used in His teachings about the Rapture that were different than the words Paul used in his two Rapture passages. Jesus in His teaching of the Rapture in both Matthew and Mark uses the word "gather" instead of "caught up" or "the dead shall rise." The Apostle Paul also used this same word "gather," *"regarding the coming of our Lord Jesus Christ and our gathering together to Him,"* to describe the Rapture when he wrote the second letter to the Thessalonians about their concerns and fears that the Rapture had already happened. The Lord gathering His people to Himself is exactly what He is doing in the Rapture. So, it is a perfectly fitting word, used by our Lord and the Apostle Paul to describe the Rapture. The second word, in referring to His people, Jesus says, "His elect" instead of "those in Christ," but Scripture will prove this word is used in several places to mean all those in Christ. Let's look at these Scriptures.

COLOSSIANS 3:11-12 (NKJV)
¹¹ where there is neither Greek nor Jew, circumcised nor uncircumcised, barbarian, Scythian, slave nor free, but Christ is all and in all.
¹² Therefore, as the elect of God, holy and beloved, put on tender mercies, kindness, humility, meekness, longsuffering;

First of all, the Apostle Paul is writing to the Colossians, a Gentile Church. He is saying Christ is all and all. It does not matter if you are Jew, or Gentile. He calls them the elect of God, holy and beloved. The word "elect" is used in this passage to describe everyone in Christ, both Jew and Gentile.

TITUS 1:1 (NKJV)

¹ Paul, a bondservant of God and an apostle of Jesus Christ, according to the faith of God's elect and the acknowledgment of the truth which accords with godliness

Again, Paul is writing to a gentile Church and identifying those of the faith as *"God's elect."* Clearly this word "elect" is used in Scripture to mean all those in Christ, both Jew and Gentile. Now that we know beyond a shadow of a doubt that Jesus is teaching about the one and only Rapture and Resurrection of the saints, let's see what else Jesus has to say about when the Rapture will take place.

MATTHEW 24:29-31 (NKJV)

²⁹ "Immediately after the tribulation of those days the sun will be darkened, and the moon will not give its light; the stars will fall from heaven, and the powers of the heavens will be shaken.

³⁰ Then the sign of the Son of Man will appear in heaven, and then all the tribes of the earth will mourn, and they will see the Son of Man coming on the clouds of heaven with power and great glory.

³¹ And He will send His angels with a great sound of a trumpet, and they will gather together His elect from the four winds, from one end of heaven to the other.

MARK 13:24-27 (NKJV)

²⁴ "But in those days, after that tribulation, the sun will be darkened, and the moon will not give its light;

²⁵ the stars of heaven will fall, and the powers in the heavens will be shaken.

²⁶ Then they will see the Son of Man coming in the clouds with great power and glory.

²⁷ And then He will send His angels, and gather together His elect from the four winds, from the farthest part of earth to the farthest part of heaven.

Jesus says in both *Matthew* and *Mark* that the Rapture is after the Tribulation! If the Rapture is after the Tribulation, it would be important for us to understand what the Tribulation is. The Lord Jesus

gives a good description of what the Tribulation is in the verses just prior to the ones we have been reading about His coming, and the Rapture. Let's read what the Lord has to say about the Tribulation.

MATTHEW 24:9-11 (NKJV)
9 "Then they will deliver you up to tribulation and kill you, and you will be hated by all nations for My name's sake.
10 And then many will be offended, will betray one another, and will hate one another.
11 Then many false prophets will rise up and deceive many.

The Lord says we are going to be hated by all nations and they are going to kill us (those who are in Christ). We know from the book of Revelation that the beast-antichrist who will rule all the nations for forty-two months during the Sixth Trumpet will make war with the saints and will eventually kill anyone who does not worship his image. Jesus says many will be offended, they will betray and hate one another. This is the falling away that Paul was talking about in *2 Thessalonians 2*. Jesus says that false prophets will rise up and deceive many. We know from *Revelation 13* that the false prophet will deceive the whole world and cause them to worship the beast-antichrist. And as we have learned from *2 Thessalonians 2*, the Rapture comes after the beast, who is the antichrist, and the falling away. Continuing Jesus' teaching on the Tribulation of the saints.

MATTHEW 24:15-18 (NKJV)
15 "Therefore when you see the 'abomination of desolation,' spoken of by Daniel the prophet, standing in the holy place" (whoever reads, let him understand),
16 "then let those who are in Judea flee to the mountains.
17 Let him who is on the housetop not go down to take anything out of his house.
18 And let him who is in the field not go back to get his clothes.

Question—What is this *"abomination of desolation"*? Why is it that people must flee to the mountains and leave their homes and properties behind?

MATTHEW 24:15 (NKJV)

¹⁵ "Therefore when you see the 'abomination of desolation,' spoken of by Daniel the prophet, standing in the holy place" (whoever reads, let him understand)

MARK 13:14 (NKJV)

¹⁴ "So when you see the 'abomination of desolation,' spoken of by Daniel the prophet, standing where it ought not" (let the reader understand)

The prophet Daniel says the abomination of desolation is set up, and Jesus, in all the Gospel accounts, says you will see it standing in the holy place where it should not be. What I want you to take notice of here is that it is standing, not sitting. Paul, when describing the antichrist, says he is sitting on a throne, exactly what you would expect a ruler to do. The abomination of desolation is set up and is standing, and that's what you would expect to be done with a statue, to set it up and for it to be standing. I believe this abomination of desolation is the image of the beast. Further evidence of this is in what we learned in the book *Revelation*, that everyone who does not worship this image will be killed. A time when the beast-antichrist rules all the nations leaving believers with nowhere to go but to have to flee their homes and property just as it says concerning the abomination of desolation. This creates the worst persecution and tribulation in history for God's people, and for anyone who does not want to worship the statue of the antichrist. Even more evidence of this is found in the following verses.

MATTHEW 24:21-22 (NKJV)

²¹ For then there will be great tribulation, such as has not been since the beginning of the world until this time, no, nor ever shall be.
²² And unless those days were shortened, no flesh would be saved; but for the elect's sake those days will be shortened.

Jesus states this is the Greatest Tribulation of all time and is so terrible if He does not shorten it no flesh would survive, providing proof that this has to be at the end. We know from Revelation that the beast's global reign during this Sixth Trumpet is only forty-two months, and this image is set up sometime after the beginning of his global reign, and the Seventh Trumpet is soon to follow. So, the Great Tribulation

Jesus taught about and the great persecution of the saints by the beast are both at the end right before the coming of Christ at the Seventh Trumpet. Since the image of the beast is a statue, and there is every indication the abomination of desolation is a statue, and they both trigger the greatest persecution causing the Greatest Tribulation of the saints ever, I believe this makes a solid case that the abomination of desolation is the image of the beast. Let's look at the final word Jesus has to say about the Tribulation period.

MATTHEW 24:23-25 (NKJV)

23 "Then if anyone says to you, 'Look, here is the Christ!' or 'There!' do not believe it.

24 For false christs and false prophets will rise and show great signs and wonders to deceive, if possible, even the elect.

25 See, I have told you beforehand.

We know the Messiah has already come and there has been, and will possibly be, more antichrist figures and false prophets. But, the antichrist and his false prophet, as it says in *Revelation 13*, will perform great signs and wonders and will deceive the whole world into worshiping the antichrist, and as Jesus says, if possible, to deceive the elect. As it says, He has told us ahead of time in Scripture so we would know and not be deceived by this beast and his false prophet. Jesus continues with this in the next verses.

MATTHEW 24:26-27 (NKJV)

26 "Therefore if they say to you, 'Look, He is in the desert!' do not go out; or 'Look, He is in the inner rooms!' do not believe it.

27 For as the lightning comes from the east and flashes to the west, so also will the coming of the Son of Man be.

Jesus makes it clear not to look for Him on the earth when He returns. He's going to light up the sky and every eye is going to see Him. After studying all three teachers of the Rapture and Resurrection, concluding with Jesus' teachings on these and the Tribulation, and now understanding what the Tribulation is, it is time to compare Jesus' teachings to the Apostle Paul in his epistles and the Apostle John in the book of *Revelation* as to when the Rapture will happen.

The Apostle Paul says in his epistles—
- The Rapture is at the coming of the Lord and is part of the Resurrection.
- The Rapture is at the Last Trumpet of God.
- The Rapture is after the coming of the beast-antichrist and the falling away of believers.
- The Apostle Paul does not teach that the Resurrection and Rapture of the saints happens at any other time outside this list.

The Apostle John in the book Revelation reveals—
- The Seventh and Last Trumpet of God is the coming of the Lord and the Resurrection of the saints, which will include the Rapture.
- The Resurrection, which includes the Rapture, is after the global reign of the beast, who is the antichrist, which occurs between the Sixth Trumpet and the Seventh and Last Trumpet.
- The beast makes war with the saints causing a terrible tribulation for the saints.
- The beast sets up an image and forces the whole world to worship the image of the beast or be executed, causing the Greatest Tribulation ever for the saints.
- The Apostle John does not teach that the Resurrection and Rapture of the saints happens at any other time outside this list.

The Lord Jesus Christ says in the Gospels—
- The Resurrection and Rapture are after the Tribulation.
- The Tribulation is a time when all nations will turn against believers.
- Warns only those who endure to the end will be saved.
- Warns about false prophets and false christs.
- Warns us not to be deceived by anyone claiming to be Christ on the earth.
- When He comes, it will be in the sky.
- Warns about the setting up of the abomination of desolation, which is the image of the beast, which causes the Greatest Tribulation of the saints in history. So terrible, if it was not shortened, no flesh would be saved.
- The Lord does not teach that the Resurrection and Rapture of the saints happens at any other time outside this list.

After listing a summary of the teachings of each of the three witnesses on the Resurrection and the Rapture, the comparison of their teachings is as follows:

— Jesus and Paul both teach that the Rapture is part of the global Resurrection of the saints.
— The Apostle Paul, the book of Revelation, and Jesus all teach that the coming of the Lord and the Resurrection, which includes the Rapture, are at the Trumpet of God, and the Apostle Paul and the book of Revelation both further expound on this and reveal that the coming of the Lord, the Resurrection and Rapture, are at the Last and Seventh Trumpet of God.
— Jesus and John in the book of Revelation say the Resurrection and Rapture are after a great persecution and tribulation of the saints. Paul says it is after the falling away, which is at least in part caused by the persecution and tribulation of believers.

After carefully studying and comparing the teachings of all three teachers of the Rapture and Resurrection, the Apostle Paul in his epistles, the Apostle John in the book of Revelation, and our Lord Jesus Christ in the Gospels, it is very clear that all three of these witnesses are in absolute agreement as to when the Rapture takes place. They do not teach that the Resurrection and Rapture happens at any other time, neither does any other Scripture teach the Rapture and Resurrection happens at any time different than what these three witnesses have said. As was said at beginning of this final section of this chapter, our Lord Jesus Christ, who is the Word of God, will get the final Word, and Jesus says the Rapture is after the Tribulation.

MATTHEW 24:29-31 (NKJV)

29 "Immediately after the tribulation of those days the sun will be darkened, and the moon will not give its light; the stars will fall from heaven, and the powers of the heavens will be shaken.

30 Then the sign of the Son of Man will appear in heaven, and then all the tribes of the earth will mourn, and they will see the Son of Man coming on the clouds of heaven with power and great glory.

³¹ And He will send His angels with a great sound of a trumpet, and they will gather together His elect from the four winds, from one end of heaven to the other.

MARK 13:24-27 (NKJV)

²⁴ "But in those days, after that tribulation, the sun will be darkened, and the moon will not give its light;
²⁵ the stars of heaven will fall, and the powers in the heavens will be shaken.
²⁶ Then they will see the Son of Man coming in the clouds with great power and glory.
²⁷ And then He will send His angels, and gather together His elect from the four winds, from the farthest part of earth to the farthest part of heaven.

I am going to say this one more time to make this point very clear; Jesus never taught that His coming and the Rapture and Resurrection are at any time other than after the Tribulation. Neither does the Apostle Paul or the Apostle John, or any other Scriptures. That is exactly what you would expect since there is one, and only one, Resurrection and Rapture of all the saints.

Summary of the answers to our question—*When is the Rapture?*

1. The Rapture is at the coming of the Lord for all His people, both those who have died and those still alive on the earth.
2. The Rapture is at the Last Trumpet of God, which is the Seventh and Last Trumpet in the book of Revelation, and the very Last Trumpet in the Bible, making it the true Last Trumpet.
3. The Rapture is at the Resurrection of the saints.
4. The Rapture is after the Tribulation, which includes the great persecution of the beast, who is the antichrist.

QUESTION 3

WHY IS THE RAPTURE WHEN IT IS?

Another way to put this is question; Why are the saints going through the Tribulation? What does the Bible have to say about the saints and the Tribulation? Let's investigate that to help us understand the answer to the question.

ACTS 14:22 (NKJV)
22 strengthening the souls of the disciples, exhorting them to continue in the faith, and saying, "We must through many tribulations enter the kingdom of God."

I PETER 4:12-13 (NKJV)
12 Beloved, do not think it strange concerning the fiery trial which is to try you, as though some strange thing happened to you;
13 but rejoice to the extent that you partake of Christ's sufferings, that when His glory is revealed, you may also be glad with exceeding joy.

The writer of Acts says we must go through tribulations. Peter says we are not to be surprised by the fiery trials, which are to try you, which means to test you. One of the meanings of "tribulation" is "trial" or "testing." When you combine the meanings of these two related verses together, they say we must go through many trials and tribulations, "tests," and to not be surprised by them but instead rejoice in them because we get to share in Christ's suffering. Tests have rewards if they are passed and consequences if they are failed. One reward is that we get to prove our love for Christ by sharing in His suffering. What are some of the other rewards saints receive for sharing in Christ's

suffering? Let's continue investigating and see what Scripture says.

ROMANS 8:17 (NIV)

¹⁷ Now if we are children, then we are heirs—heirs of God and co-heirs with Christ, if indeed we share in his sufferings in order that we may also share in his glory.

This verse says that sharing in Christ's suffering is what allows us to share in His Glory, and it implies that suffering is not only the way to share in His glory, but the more we share in His suffering the more we will share in His glory. Which would explain why Peter said to rejoice in the fact that you get to share in Christ's suffering, because he knew it meant being worthy to share in His glory. The next Scripture verses expound on this.

I TIMOTHY 2:11-12 (KJV)

¹¹ It is a faithful saying: For if we be dead with him, we shall also live with him:
¹² If we suffer, we shall also reign with him: if we deny him, he also will deny us:

This verse says if we suffer with Him, we will rule with Him. Suffering with Christ gives us an opportunity to receive the highest possible reward in heaven, which is to rule with Christ. If you remember in the first Resurrection in *Revelation*, those who suffered under the beast were specifically mentioned as reigning with Christ for a thousand years. I believe they will not be the only ones, because many have suffered for Christ over the millenniums, but the last days saints that go through the Great Tribulation at the time of the beast will have possibly suffered more since it is going to be the Greatest Tribulation of the saints in the history of the world. Another note, if you remember from *Hebrews 11*, it said they did not accept deliverance so they would have a better Resurrection, which is when we will all receive our reward, inheritance, and our position in heaven. So, these verses we have studied paint a clear picture, there is a direct relationship between how much we suffer and how much glory we will receive, including the highest honor of ruling with Christ. This means if our eyes, our focus, is on heaven, suffering and tribulation is something to be desired. Like Peter said, it is something to rejoice and be happy about. Let's look what Jesus has to say about tribulation and the reward for suffering it.

JOHN 16:33 (NKJV)

³³ These things I have spoken to you, that in Me you may have peace. In the world you will have tribulation; but be of good cheer, I have overcome the world.

Just like Peter and Paul in the previous passages, Jesus says we will have tribulation in the world, and like Peter, He also says to be happy, but gives a different reason, and that is because He has overcome the world. What does Jesus mean when He encourages us to be of good cheer because He has overcome the world? This is what I believe, because He overcame the world as a man, He knows what it takes to overcome our weaknesses and can now help us overcome by giving us His Holy Spirit and grace in proportion to what we need to overcome. He also lived a perfect overcomers life to show us how to overcome. What was that overcomers life? It is the life of the cross, which is a life of sacrifice and suffering. Let's see what Jesus has to say about the rewards of going through tribulation and being an overcomer in the book of *Revelation*.

REVELATION 2:10 (NKJV)

¹⁰ Do not fear any of those things which you are about to suffer. Indeed, the devil is about to throw some of you into prison, that you may be tested, and you will have tribulation ten days. Be faithful until death, and I will give you the crown of life.

In this verse, Jesus describes tribulation as a test, and a reward for passing the test in this case is the crown of life. A crown represents authority and a treasure to possess. Jesus also commands them not fear. He would not have told them not to fear if they could not endure this trial and endure it without fear. He also encourages them by telling them how long the Tribulation will last, which is only ten days. That really is an encouragement because going into tribulation knowing how long it is going to last, in this case only ten days, and that it is not going to go on and on with no end in sight, will help them to not give up and to endure to the end.

REVELATION 2:26 (NKJV)

²⁶ And he who overcomes, and keeps My works until the end, to him I will give power over the nations—

In this promise, Jesus says those who overcome and endure to the end will be given authority to rule the nations. In the Tribulation, the saints will be treated as enemies of the world and will be hated by all the nations, but in a very short time, those saints will be ruling the nations and those who hated them will be destroyed.

REVELATION 3:21 (NKJV)

²¹ To him who overcomes I will grant to sit with Me on My throne, as I also overcame and sat down with My Father on His throne.

"Wow" is all I can say here. To sit with Christ on His throne must be the highest honor granted to any created being. We have learned there is a direct relationship between our suffering and our reward and glory in heaven, and the greater the suffering, the greater the reward and glory. After what we learned about how terrible the Great Tribulation is, to the saints who have to go through the Greatest Tribulation and suffering in the history of world it would seem to be a punishment, but it is not. Instead it is possibly the greatest opportunity for the last days saints, more any other generation, to share in Christ's suffering, and then as a reward, to share in His authority and rule and rein with Him. There are Scriptures that describe Christ's attitude towards the suffering He would have to endure on the cross for us. Let look at that Scripture.

HEBREWS 12:2 (NKJV)

² looking unto Jesus, the author and finisher of our faith, who for the joy that was set before Him endured the cross, despising the shame, and has sat down at the right hand of the throne of God.

Think about this; He was the Son of God, but for the joy and reward set before Him, He endured the terrible scourging, beatings, mocking, and the shame that ended with His death on the cross. He despised the shame for the joy and reward set before Him. He was showing us how to endure the sufferings we will face by putting our

eyes on Him, heaven, and our everlasting reward.

I PETER 4:1-2 (NKJV)
¹ Therefore, since Christ suffered for us in the flesh, arm yourselves also with the same mind, for he who has suffered in the flesh has ceased from sin,
² that he no longer should live the rest of his time in the flesh for the lusts of men, but for the will of God.

This verse says to arm ourselves with a mind to suffer We have some understanding of this because that is what we have been learning in this section. Be joyful because Christ has overcome the world and will help us to overcome. Do not fear the test of tribulation because we know Christ, who is the author and finisher of our faith, will get us through it if we trust Him instead of giving in to fear. Like Christ, look to the joy of great reward and glory that suffering brings us, remembering that with more suffering there is greater reward and glory, even the glory of possibly sitting in Christ's throne with Him if we live our lives for the will of God and not the lusts of men. If we can set our hearts and minds to do these things, we can endure the trials and tribulations to come. As the Scripture says, arm yourself with a mind of suffering. One final instruction on how to do this is from the Lord Jesus Christ.

LUKE 9:23 (NKJV)
²³ Then He said to them all, "If anyone desires to come after Me, let him deny himself, and take up his cross daily, and follow Me."

As if the awesome reward of eternal life and ruling with Christ is not enough, the Tribulation is not all suffering. As we have been learning, eternal authority is directly related to suffering, and not just eternal authority but real kingdom authority right here on the earth. The Apostle Paul confirmed his kingdom authority to the Churches through his suffering. Jesus taught that at the time of the harvest both the wheat and tares, the sons of God and the sons of the devil, will be mature. The last days saints will be spiritually mature, and that combined with great suffering, many are going to walk in great kingdom authority and power with some possibly walking in the greater works that Jesus taught about. Daniel also wrote about this.

DANIEL 11:32 (NKJV)

³² Those who do wickedly against the covenant he shall corrupt with flattery; but the people who know their God shall be strong, and carry out great exploits.

"Great exploits" means great heroic acts. Some of the last days saints are going to be great heroes working great miracles by the power of God. There is no question that the Tribulation is going to be a terrible time, but if we prepare for this time, like a soldier who prepares for battle, instead of looking at these times as something to dread we can look at them as an opportunity for great reward and victory.

We learned how the Tribulation is a time of testing, and if we endure, we will not only inherit eternal life but also gain a better inheritance at the Resurrection. The Tribulation is not just for the saints to have a better inheritance at the Resurrection. As with all of creation, its primary purpose is for the glory of the Lord. In *Job 1:8,* the Lord was boasting about the righteousness of His servant Job to His arch enemy Satan. *Job 1:9-11,* the devil challenges God that Job was not truly righteous and only lives a righteous life because of all the blessing and protection he has received from the Lord. So, in *Job 1:12* the Lord allows Job to be tested, and in this test Job's character was truly revealed and God was glorified in His servant Job, and He restored double of all he had lost. The point is, when the saints pass the test of tribulation, not only is their character proven but they glorify God in a way that only the test of tribulation can glorify Him, and that's why the rewards for passing the test of tribulation are so great. The Great Tribulation is not the worst thing to happen to God's people, but rather the greatest opportunity for God to prove the character of His people and for His people to glorify Him and be counted worthy to rule and rein with Him. Job was a mature saint, and at the end of the age the saints should also be mature saints. There is another reason that the Tribulation is for the Lord's sake; the Tribulation is the time of the harvest. In *Matthew 13:37-43,* Jesus taught the wheat, the sons of God, and the tares, the sons of the devil, will mature together until the time of the harvest. When the wheat and the tares grow together there is going to be some entanglement and they will need to be separated. The Tribulation is when the separation takes place, it will reveal the true and mature

saints and remove the tares, the hypocrites and the lukewarm, *Revelation 3:16*, from His bride. Scripture says the Lord is coming back for a bride that has made herself ready.

REVELATION 19:7-8 (NKJV)

7 Let us be glad and rejoice and give Him glory, for the marriage of the Lamb has come, and His wife has made herself ready."
8 And to her it was granted to be arrayed in fine linen, clean and bright, for the fine linen is the righteous acts of the saints.

How does the Tribulation help the bride make herself ready for Christ? *Romans 5:3-5* provides an answer.

ROMANS 5:3-5 (NKJV)

3 And not only that, but we also glory in tribulations, knowing that tribulation produces perseverance;
4 and perseverance, character; and character, hope.
5 Now hope does not disappoint, because the love of God has been poured out in our hearts by the Holy Spirit who was given to us.

This passage says tribulation produces perseverance, and perseverance produces character, and character produces hope, and that hope is realized because our hearts are filled with the love of God by the Holy Spirit, giving evidence that the character of Christ is being developed in all of us. What are some other ways the Tribulation helps the bride prepare herself for Christ?

I JOHN 3:2-3 (NKJV)

2 Beloved, now we are children of God; and it has not yet been revealed what we shall be, but we know that when He is revealed, we shall be like Him, for we shall see Him as He is.
3 And everyone who has this hope in Him purifies himself, just as He is pure.

The previous passage says tribulation produces perseverance, character, and hope, and these verses say that hope causes us to purify ourselves so that we can be like Him. The hope that comes from the character developed by tribulation also causes us to purify ourselves so we can be like Christ. There is another way the Tribulation purifies and prepares the bride for Christ in *Matthew 25*. Jesus teaches about the ten virgins, which represent the bride of Christ, waiting for Christ during the long dark night of the Great Tribulation. Five of them fell away and went back to the world before the Lord came and received His bride, which was half of them. The long dark night of the Great Tribulation proved and purified the character of those truly devoted to Christ and it also exposed and proved the lack of devotion of those who did not truly love Him.

Tribulation is to prepare and purify a bride for Christ that truly loves Him and is completely devoted to Him. The book of Daniel also teaches about God's people being purified in the Tribulation.

DANIEL 12:10 (NKJV)
¹⁰ Many shall be purified, made white, and refined, but the wicked shall do wickedly; and none of the wicked shall understand, but the wise shall understand.

This is what Jesus said about the those who have a pure heart.

MATTHEW 5:8 (NKJV)
⁸ Blessed are the pure in heart, For they shall see God.

Scripture says that Moses was the most humble man on earth and that he experienced regular face to face encounters with God. Why is being humble, or more correctly, humbling ourselves as Jesus commanded, the way to purify our hearts? When we truly humble ourselves, we let go of self-importance and increase the value, the treasure, of God and others in our hearts. In other words, decreasing self makes more room in our hearts to love God and others.

1 JOHN 3:2 (NKJV)
² but we know that when He is revealed, we shall be like Him, for we shall see Him as He is.

John says when we truly see Him as He is, we will be like Him. He is love, and true love is the greatest longing and desire of all

mankind. Once our hearts are pure enough to see that the Lord is pure love, we will be able to see He really is the true desire of our hearts, and being our greatest desire, He will become our greatest love. What we love the most we will purposely pursue the most, our hearts will move us to put our time and devotion into seeking the Lord more than anything else because He is who we love the most. We become what we have devoted our lives to becoming, so the more we seek the Lord with all our heart, the more and more we will become like Him.

Tribulation will test what is in our hearts. If our hearts are not filled with the love of God, we will fall away in the time of testing. But if our primary devotion is to the Lord, it will purify what is left that is not devoted to the Lord. That's why the Lord allows tribulation in our lives in the first place. It is to help purify our hearts of what is not devoted to Him and to purge His Church of the truly undevoted, as well as wake up some that have gone to sleep and need to repent before it is too late. We need to heed these lesser tribulations while there is still time because the Great Tribulation will purge the undevoted and lukewarm. Now is the time to seek the Lord and purify our hearts, and then He can finish that work with the Great Tribulation if we are alive to see it. There is one more reason God allows the saints to go through tribulation, and that is for His Glory. The following verses reveal this truth.

MATTHEW 5:10-12 (NKJV)
10 Blessed are those who are persecuted for righteousness' sake,
For theirs is the kingdom of heaven.
11 Blessed are you when they revile and persecute you, and say all kinds of evil against you falsely for My sake.
12 Rejoice and be exceedingly glad, for great is your reward in heaven, for so they persecuted the prophets who were before you.

1 PETER 4:14 (NKJV)
14 If you are reproached for the name of Christ, blessed are you, for the Spirit of glory and of God rests upon you. On their part He is blasphemed, but on your part He is glorified.

God is glorified when we suffer for Him. If we live righteously when it is easy to do so, God only receives a little glory, but if we continue walking in godliness when we are persecuted, He is greatly glorified before His Son and Spirit, before His Angels, before men who understand the truth, before the great cloud of witnesses in heaven and before His enemies. This may be the one time we can actually give something to God. And he rewards us greatly for it.

To summarize, tribulation and the Great Tribulation are times that the bride has the greatest opportunity to prepare herself and prove her love and devotion to her Beloved and to purify the bride of Christ so He can receive His bride, as it says in *Revelation 19:7*, that she has made herself ready. It is also the time when the saints can glorify God the most!

Another question that needs to be answered—Does Scripture reveal that some of the saints will escape and be protected during the time of the Great Tribulation? Yes, it does. There are two groups of people that Scripture specifically describes who are protected during the Great Tribulation, and also provides answers to why they are protected in *Revelation 2 and 3*. The Lord addresses the seven Churches of Asia with the letters written to each Church. Of the seven Churches, the Church of Philadelphia is the only Church that is given the promise to be protected from the Great Tribulation.

REVELATION 3:7, 10 (NKJV)
7 "And to the angel of the Church in Philadelphia write,
10 Because you have kept My command to persevere, I also will keep you from the hour of trial which shall come upon the whole world, to test those who dwell on the earth.

The Church in Philadelphia is told, because they obeyed and persevered, they would be kept from the hour of trial that comes over the whole world to test the people of the earth. I believe this hour (time) of trial and testing of the whole world is the Great Tribulation because the Great Tribulation is the only time in Scripture when the entire world is being tested. The Scripture says because they obeyed and persevered, which means to endure to the end. What did they persevere through? The answer is in what they are being kept from, trial and

testing, in other words, tribulation. This Scripture says because they obeyed and endured the trial and testing of tribulation to the end of it, they would be kept from the Great Tribulation to come upon the whole world.

Is persevering through tribulation the only reason they are kept from the Great Tribulation? Or is there is more to it? When addressing the seven Churches of Asia, the Lord does bring a single charge against the Church of Philadelphia, but He mentions an issue with most of the other Churches and with many of them He says He has something against them. How does that explain why they are kept from the Great Tribulation? As the Scripture said, the Tribulation is a trial, a test. With a test, you either pass or fail. The Church of Philadelphia had no charges against them after their trial and testing, so they passed the test. To just endure tribulation is not enough to be kept from future tribulation, only by passing the test of the Tribulation to the Lord's satisfaction does one qualify to not have to endure the test of tribulation again. This brings up another question; is this promise just to the Church of Philadelphia? I do not believe so. Near the end of every letter to the seven Churches, it says this *"He who has an ear, let him hear what the Spirit says to the Churches."* Notice it says, *"to the Churches,"* meaning all the Churches, not just one, then followed by an overcomer promise, a different promise to each Church that in many cases seems to be related to the rebukes and promises given in the letter to that individual Church. I believe since the Lord started these promises with addressing all the Churches, all the promises are for all the Churches and individual saints who qualify for the promises. I believe the same is true for the rebukes and warnings in those letters, they apply to all the Churches and saints.

With that, I believe we can now understand that the promise of being kept from the trial and testing of the Great Tribulation is not limited to the Church of Philadelphia but is for all the Churches and saints who obey, persevere, and pass the testing of tribulation in a way that is acceptable to the Lord to qualify them to be kept from the Great Tribulation. Remember, tribulation is not just to prove ourselves worthy to rule with Christ, but it is also to finish purifying our hearts of any lack of devotion to the Lord. Scripture does not give what is an acceptable test of tribulation required to qualify escaping the Great

Tribulation, but one thing we can do is embrace all tribulation as a test from the Lord and do our best to pass the test. We may not suffer enough tribulation to qualify to escape the Great Tribulation, but if we do embrace tribulations as they come and remember the suffering they bring is more to qualify us to rule with Christ than to escape the Great Tribulation, we will have put on a mindset to suffer, as Scripture says to do, and we will be much better prepared to endure and pass the test of the Great Tribulation.

Speaking of the time of the Great Tribulation, it is at the end of the age, and the Church of Philadelphia was at the beginning of the Church age, and in no way could the saints in the Church at that time be alive during the Great Tribulation. So why did the Lord give this promise to the Church of Philadelphia? I believe the Lord gave this promise to the Church of Philadelphia because they qualified to be kept from the Great Tribulation and He wanted them to know that, and for future generations of the Church to understand it. I also believe the Lord gave this promise to the Church of Philadelphia directly because even though the early Church would not go through the Great Tribulation, they did experience a lot of tribulation in their time, and since the Church of Philadelphia qualified to be kept from the Great Tribulation, they would qualify to be kept from future tribulation during their lifetime. In fact, one of the reasons there is a Rapture of the saints still alive at the Lord's coming is because there will be saints who get through the Great Tribulation without being killed. This is no human achievable feat, even the Lord Himself said he has to shorten those days, otherwise no flesh would be saved, *Matthew 24:22*. It is very likely many of the saints who make it to the end of the Great Tribulation and are Raptured were kept and protected during the Great Tribulation.

The second group of saints to be protected from the Great Tribulation is found in *Revelation 12* and *Daniel 12*. This one requires some in-depth study of Scripture to understand who these people are.

REVELATION 12:1 (NKJV)
[1] Now a great sign appeared in heaven: a woman clothed with the sun, with the moon under her feet, and on her head a garland of twelve stars.

To understand who this woman is, we need to search the Scriptures and what Scriptures have to say about the signs given to describe this woman. It says she is clothed with the sun, with the moon under her feet and a garland of twelve stars on her head. One clue is the garland of twelve stars. Are twelve stars mentioned anywhere else in Scripture? Not exactly, but the number twelve is the number of the twelve tribes of Israel. Is there a Scripture that describes the twelve tribes of Israel as stars? Yes, in *Genesis 37*.

GENESIS 37:9-11 (NKJV)

9 Then he dreamed still another dream and told it to his brothers, and said, "Look, I have dreamed another dream. And this time, the sun, the moon, and the eleven stars bowed down to me."
10 So he told it to his father and his brothers; and his father rebuked him and said to him, "What is this dream that you have dreamed? Shall your mother and I and your brothers indeed come to bow down to the earth before you?"
11 And his brothers envied him, but his father kept the matter in mind.

Joseph describes a dream he had to his father Jacob, who is Israel, and his eleven brothers. His father rebukes him because he understood the significance of this dream, the sun represented Jacob, the moon Joseph's mother and the eleven stars his eleven brothers, and in the dream they all bow down to him. This verse only describes eleven stars as the sons of Jacob, who become the tribes of Israel, but Joseph who had the dream is also a son of Jacob and a tribe of Israel, making him a twelfth star. I believe since there are no other Scriptures that describe twelve stars that the twelve stars on the woman's head in *Revelation 12:1* are the twelve tribes of Israel. Continuing the comparison of the woman in *Revelation 12* and Joseph's dream, in his dream the sun represents Jacob his father, and the moon his mother.

REVELATION 12:1 (NKJV)

1 Now a great sign appeared in heaven: a woman clothed with the sun, with the moon under her feet, and on her head a garland of twelve stars.

The woman is clothed with the sun. How can Jacob as the sun

clothe a woman? Clothing is a covering, and Scripture says a husband is a covering for his wife. Why would the moon, which in Joseph's dream presents the mother of Israel, be under her feet? Since this woman appears as a mother.

REVELATION 12:2 (NKJV)
² Then being with child, she cried out in labor and in pain to give birth.

This is what I believe being under someone's feet represents— being under their authority. So, if the moon under her feet is the mothers of Israel being under her authority, then this woman represents a great mother in Israel with great authority. Continuing this passage about the woman.

REVELATION 12:3-5 (NKJV)
³ And another sign appeared in heaven: behold, a great, fiery red dragon having seven heads and ten horns, and seven diadems on his heads.
⁴ His tail drew a third of the stars of heaven and threw them to the earth. And the dragon stood before the woman who was ready to give birth, to devour her Child as soon as it was born.
⁵ She bore a male Child who was to rule all nations with a rod of iron. And her Child was caught up to God and His throne.

These verses describe the woman giving birth to a male Child who will rule all the nations with a rod of iron and is caught up to God's throne. The dragon, who is the devil, *Revelation 12:9*, tries to devour her Child as soon as it He born. There are only two male children in all of Scripture that the devil tried to devour as soon as, or soon after, they were born, and they are Jesus and Moses. To help better understand who this woman is, we need to know who this male Child is who will rule all the nations with a rod of iron and is caught up to God's throne.

MARK 16:19 (NKJV)
¹⁹ So then, after the Lord had spoken to them, He was received up into heaven, and sat down at the right hand of God.

This verse shows Christ, who is the male Child, was caught up to heaven and sat down at the right-hand of God's throne. There are no other Scriptures of anyone being caught up to God's throne except Jesus Christ. I believe the next verse gives further proof that Jesus is the male Child that was caught up to God's throne and rules all the nations with a rod of iron.

REVELATION 19:15 (NKJV)

15 Now out of His mouth goes a sharp sword, that with it He should strike the nations. And He Himself will rule them with a rod of iron. He Himself treads the winepress of the fierceness and wrath of Almighty God.

This Scripture is describing Christ's return to the earth and shows it is Christ Himself who will rule the nations with a rod of iron, leaving no doubt who the male child is in *Revelation 12:5,* a male Child who was to rule all the nations with a rod of iron. The description of the woman in *Revelation 12:1* indicates to the woman being Israel, and Israel, as with many nations, is often referred to in the feminine, like <u>her</u> or <u>she</u>. But *Revelation 12:2,4-5* describe the woman as being the mother of a male Child who is Jesus Christ, His mother is Mary. How is it possible for this woman to be both Israel and Mary? I believe Scripture provides a good explanation for this.

REVELATION 12:1 (NKJV)

1 Now a great sign appeared in heaven: a woman clothed with the sun, with the moon under her feet, and on her head a garland of twelve stars.

The very first thing the Scripture says about this woman is she appears as a great sign in heaven. Since this woman is revealed as sign, she can represent more than just a woman, and Scripture does reveal she is both Israel and Mary.

Question—Does this woman ultimately represent Israel or Mary? To answer this question, we will continue to read what *Revelation 12* has to say about this woman.

REVELATION 12:6,13-14 (NKJV)

6 Then the woman fled into the wilderness, where she has a place prepared by God, that they should feed her there one thousand two hundred and sixty days

13 Now when the dragon saw that he had been cast to the earth, he persecuted the woman who gave birth to the male Child.

14 But the woman was given two wings of a great eagle, that she might fly into the wilderness to her place, where she is nourished for a time and times and half a time, from the presence of the serpent.

We can see from these verses that the woman flies into the wilderness with help from God because she was *"given two wings of a great eagle"* to fly to a place prepared by God where she is fed and nourished for, for one-thousand-two-hundred-and-sixty days, which is *a time and times and half a time*, which is three-and-a-half years. I believe the reason the measure of time is given in two different ways is so it cannot be changed into a different measure of time. So why is this woman carried into the wilderness to be cared for, for three-and-a-half years from the dragon? The next verses we are going to read in this chapter about the dragon will help us understand that.

REVELATION 12:9,12 (NKJV)

9 So the great dragon was cast out, that serpent of old, called the Devil and Satan, who deceives the whole world; he was cast to the earth, and his angels were cast out with him.

12 Therefore rejoice, O heavens, and you who dwell in them! Woe to the inhabitants of the earth and the sea! For the devil has come down to you, having great wrath, because he knows that he has a short time."

The dragon, who is the devil, who is also called Satan, is cast down to the earth and he has great wrath. His wrath is so great that the voice in heaven says, *"Woe to the to the inhabitants of the earth,"* and the reason his wrath is so great is because he knows his time is short, meaning he is just about out of time. This can only mean one thing; The return of Christ is near, which is at the Seventh Trumpet. Remember, we learned the beast who is the antichrist's three-and-a-half-year global

rein is during the Sixth Trumpet and ends at the Seventh Trumpet when Christ comes and resurrects and Raptures His people. So, with this being the end of the dragon's time on earth, and the three-and-a-half-year global rein of the beast is at the end of Satan's time on the earth, we can conclude that the one-thousand-two-hundred-and-sixty days (three-and-a-half years) that the woman flies into the wilderness to be protected from the dragon is the same three-and-a-half years of the beast-antichrist's global rein, which is the Great Tribulation. We know this woman is protected in the wilderness by God during the Great Tribulation, and we know Mary is not on the earth during the Great Tribulation, though Joseph, herself and baby Jesus fled to Egypt by God's direction to protect baby Jesus. Since Mary is not the woman protected from the dragon and the beast during the Great Tribulation, I believe we can conclude that Israel is ultimately who this woman represents. This sign of the woman as Mary also represents Israel. Mary is the woman who gave birth to Jesus, but Israel is the nation that Christ was born into, making Israel, from a national perspective, the mother of the Messiah (Christ) as well. Since the sign of the woman ultimately represents Israel, why does it also represent Mary? Reading the rest of the chapter about the woman and the dragon answers that question.

REVELATION 12:14-17 (NKJV)

14 But the woman was given two wings of a great eagle, that she might fly into the wilderness to her place, where she is nourished for a time and times and half a time, from the presence of the serpent.

15 Then from his mouth the serpent spewed water like a river, to overtake the woman and sweep her away with the torrent.

16 But the earth helped the woman by opening its mouth and swallowing the river that the dragon had spewed out of his mouth.

17 Then the dragon was enraged at the woman and went off to wage war against the rest of her offspring—those who keep God's commands and hold fast their testimony about Jesus.

The dragon tries to destroy the woman as she goes to the place prepared to protect her, but God uses the earth to swallow up the dragon's final attempt to destroy her. Then the Dragon, full of rage, goes off to make war with the rest of her offspring, *"those who keep God's commands and hold fast their testimony about Jesus."* In this last sentence, *"hold fast their testimony about Jesus,"* Israel is not just the nation that brought forth the Messiah (Christ), she is also the nation that gave birth to Christianity, so if Israel is carried off then the rest of her offspring are Christians. And if her offspring are Christians then the Israel that is carried off must be the Messianic 'Christian' Israel. Now we understand why the revelation of this woman representing Israel was also represented by Mary giving birth to the male Child, who is Jesus the Messiah, because this woman does not represent the whole nation of Israel but only Messianic 'Christian' Israel. So, it is the Messianic 'Christian' Israel that is carried off and protected for one-thousand-two-hundred-and-sixty days, the three-and-a-half-years of the Great Tribulation. *Daniel 12* confirms this.

DANIEL 12:1 (NKJV)
[1] "At that time Michael shall stand up, The great prince who stands watch over the sons of your people; And there shall be a time of trouble, Such as never was since there was a nation,
Even to that time. And at that time your people shall be delivered, Everyone who is found written in the book.

Daniel is told that the Archangel Michael who protects the people, Daniel's people, the people of Israel, will stand up at a time when there will be trouble worse than any time since there has been a nation. This is the time of the Great Tribulation taught by Jesus in the Gospels, and the time of the forty-two-month (three-and-a-half year) global reign of the beast, who is the antichrist, and his war against the saints in *Revelation 13* and *Daniel 7*, which is the primary cause of the Tribulation of the saints. Then Daniel is told his people, who is Israel, that every one of them who is found in the book of life will be delivered, which means escape and be protected from that time of great trouble. Not all of Israel is in the book of life, only those who have received the Messiah, who is Christ, will be delivered from the Great Tribulation. This confirms what we have learned from *Revelation 12* that Messianic Israel will be delivered, escape, and be protected during the Great Tribulation caused by the dragon and the beast. This brings up another

question—Why is the Messianic Christian Israel protected during the Great Tribulation? I can think of two good reasons why God has chosen to do this.

1. As we learned from an earlier chapter in *Revelation*, those who have already suffered a great tribulation may qualify to be protected during the Great Tribulation. With Israel and Jerusalem being the main focus of the beast during his rise to power and global conquest, it is highly likely that the Messianic Jews in Israel have already suffered greatly.

2. At the time of Messianic Israel's deliverance, the antichrist has just begun his forty-two-month global reign from Jerusalem and his all-out war against all saints, as described in *Revelation 13:5-8*, *Daniel 7:21-22*, *Daniel 12:7* and *2 Thessalonians 2:4*. With the Messianic Jews living in Jerusalem, and Israel literally at ground zero, they would no doubt suffer the Greatest Tribulation and would very likely be quickly wiped out if they were not delivered.

There is one more verse in Scripture that mentions some of the saints escaping the Tribulation. Before looking at that verse, let's review what Scripture says about the saints going through the Tribulation.

MATTHEW 24:9-10, 12-13 (NKJV)

9 "Then they will deliver you up to tribulation and kill you, and you will be hated by all nations for My name's sake.
10 And then many will be offended, will betray one another, and will hate one another.
12 And because lawlessness will abound, the love of many will grow cold.
13 But he who endures to the end shall be saved.

MARK 13:11-13 (NKJV)

11 But when they arrest you and deliver you up, do not worry beforehand, or premeditate what you will speak. But whatever is given you in that hour, speak that; for it is not you who speak, but the Holy Spirit.
12 Now brother will betray brother to death, and a father his child; and children will rise up against parents and cause them to be put to death.

¹³ And you will be hated by all for My name's sake. But he who endures to the end shall be saved.

LUKE 21:16-19 (NKJV)

¹⁶ You will be betrayed even by parents and brothers, relatives and friends; and they will put some of you to death.
¹⁷ And you will be hated by all for My name's sake.
¹⁸ But not a hair of your head shall be lost.
¹⁹ By your patience possess your souls.

In these three Gospel passages, the Lord teaches about the Tribulation and what the saints will go through during the Tribulation. He said they will be hated by all the nations, they will be betrayed, in some cases by their own family members, they will be arrested, and some will be killed. When they speak after being arrested, the Holy Spirit will give them words to speak. Lawlessness will overtake the world and the love of many will grow cold, but those who endure to the end will be saved. *Luke 21:19* says this in a slightly different way, *"by your patience you will possess your souls."* Patience here means to endure. In *1 Corinthians 13*, the very first quality of love is patience. These three passages reveal the saints are going through the Tribulation, and they will have to endure to the end, whether that end is death or the coming of Christ. In the message, Jesus taught about the Tribulation in the Gospel of Luke, only Jesus says this—

LUKE 21:36 (NKJV)

³⁶ Watch therefore, and pray always that you may be counted worthy to escape all these things that will come to pass, and to stand before the Son of Man."

This verse says to watch and pray that you may be counted worthy to escape the Tribulation and stand before the Son of Man. Notice it does not just say to escape, but also to stand before Christ when He comes. We know those who fall away during the Tribulation will be like the five foolish virgins in *Matthew 25* who go back to the world and will not go in with Christ when He comes. Whether we endure or escape the Tribulation, what is infinitely and eternally more important is to be worthy to stand before Christ when He comes. Having already learned that there will be some who will escape the

Tribulation, one group are those who have already endured enough tribulation and passed the test of their tribulation, and God in His grace and mercy is not going to make them go through it again. Just like the ones worthy to escape the Tribulation described in *Hebrews 11:35*, *"Others were tortured, not accepting deliverance, that they might obtain a better Resurrection,"* some may choose to endure more tribulation to receive a greater inheritance at the Resurrection. It is very likely most, if not all, who will be counted worthy to escape the Great Tribulation will understand the signs of the times and know that the end is very near and may choose to suffer instead of escape. Unlike the five foolish virgins who go back to the world, the five wise virgins know there is no world to go back to. I believe the word "escape" in this verse may also refer to those who escape the falling away during the Tribulation and testing and make it to the end to be counted worthy to stand before Christ at His coming.

There are two keys given in this verse on how to escape the Tribulation, whether that is to be protected from it or have to endure to the end. Those keys are to watch and pray always. Jesus gave many signs to watch for in *Matthew 24*, *Mark 13*, and *Luke 21*, by knowing and carefully watching the signs we will know the end is drawing near, and that will also help us to stay in the fear of the Lord and continue to walk in holiness and not fall away, lest that time catch us by surprise.

LUKE 21:34 (NKJV)

34 "But take heed to yourselves, lest your hearts be weighed down with carousing, drunkenness, and cares of this life, and that Day come on you unexpectedly.

The second key is to pray always. This continuous prayer life needs to be established before the Tribulation. True Christianity is an intimate relationship with Christ, and prayer and obedience are how we deepen that relationship. Our relationship with Him as His bride, and He as our Bridegroom, reveals that our relationship with Him should be a very intimate relationship. *Psalm 91* speaks about the protection of those who dwell in the secret place of a very close and intimate relationship with the Lord. Another way that prayer can help us endure or escape the Tribulation is when Jesus taught His disciples to pray, the prayer He taught included *"lead us not into temptation but deliver us from evil."* Jesus taught to pray that we would not be led into temptation because He knows the devil is always trying to get permission to test us beyond our limits. When the Lord tests us, it is for our good and for promotion. All the saints need to put these keys into practice and make them a significant part of their life before the Great Tribulation.

There are a lot more Scriptures that describe the antichrist making war with the saints than there are Scriptures describing the saints escaping and being protected from the Great Tribulation. One thing is for sure, the more we prepare ourselves to endure tribulation by putting on a mindset to suffer and embrace tribulation as the Lord allows it in our life as a test to pass, the greater our chances are of not only enduring the Great Tribulation but also possibly escaping some or all of it. Remember, the Lord's intent of tribulation for those that are truly devoted to Him, and therefore truly His, is for their good, for their blessing, increased inheritance, and promotion, even up to ruling with Him and sitting on His throne with Him.

WHEN IS THE RAPTURE?

PT. 2

We answered the question *"When is the Rapture?"* and Jesus got the final word. As we were learning about when the Rapture takes place, we learned that there is more than just one answer to this question. If a single answer is given, then Jesus gets the final word, the Rapture is after the Tribulation. This alone gives us some understanding of what will take place before the Rapture, and adding the other answers together, it is at the last Trumpet of God and at the time of the Resurrection of the saints. All these combined give us a good understanding of when the Rapture will happen, but they do not give us the whole picture. There is more we need to learn about when the Rapture takes place and all the events that will lead up to it. I want to cover why the Rapture is after the Tribulation before covering the rest of what I strongly believe is important for the saints to know. Some of what we still need to learn will come from the trumpet judgements.

When we started to answer the question *"When is the Rapture?"* I said, since the Rapture is at the last Trumpet of a series of trumpets, the preceding trumpets, when sounded, would have events that follow and would give us some knowledge about the signs of the times leading up to the Rapture. We looked at some of what is happening during the Sixth Trumpet, that's where we learned about the beast, the false prophet and the abomination of desolation, which is the image of the beast, and I believe that may be one, if not the most important, thing we needed to understand about what leads up to the Rapture and Resurrection. The other Trumpets individually, and together, hold some very important information that God's people should understand about what leads up to the Rapture. Since the Tribulation is before the Rapture, looking at what leads up to the Tribulation and the trumpet judgements will give us a better understanding of all the signs and events that will lead up to the Rapture. Jesus taught about the signs that lead up to the Tribulation in the Gospels.

SIGNS BEFORE THE TRIBULATION

MATTHEW 24:4-9 (NKJV)

4 And Jesus answered and said to them: "Take heed that no one deceives you.

5 For many will come in My name, saying, 'I am the Christ,' and will deceive many.

6 And you will hear of wars and rumors of wars. See that you are not troubled; for all these things must come to pass, but the end is not yet.

7 For nation will rise against nation, and kingdom against kingdom. And there will be famines, pestilences, and earthquakes in various places.

8 All these are the beginning of sorrows.

9 "Then they will deliver you up to tribulation and kill you, and you will be hated by all nations for My name's sake.

Jesus says there will be many false christs, wars, famine, pestilence and earthquakes in various places before the Tribulation. He says to not be troubled because these things must happen, but the end is not yet, all these are the beginning of sorrows. Wars, famine, pestilence and earthquakes have occurred throughout human history, what makes these different? Jesus says, nation will rise against nation and kingdom against kingdom, indicating an increase in war, even world wars. This is followed by famines, pestilence and earthquakes in various places, indicating these will also be increasing. To summarize, Jesus says there will be an increase in false christs, wars, famines, pestilence and earthquakes in various places. These are the beginning of sorrows and are before the Tribulation and the end.

THE SCROLL WITH SEVEN SEALS

The Seven Trumpets are inside a scroll with Seven Seals on it. The first four seals on the scroll, revealed in visions given to John about what Jesus was teaching in *Matthew 24:4-9,* is released on the earth.

THE LAMB TAKES THE SCROLL

REVELATION 5:1 (NKJV)
¹ And I saw in the right hand of Him who sat on the throne a scroll written inside and on the back, sealed with seven seals.

God the Father is sitting on His throne holding the scroll sealed with Seven Seals. *Verses 2-5* declare that Jesus Christ, the Lion of the tribe of Judah, has prevailed and is the only one in heaven, earth, and under the earth worthy to open the scroll and loose its seven seals.

REVELATION 5:6-7 (NKJV)
⁶ And I looked, and behold, in the midst of the throne and of the four living creatures, and in the midst of the elders, stood a Lamb as though it had been slain, having seven horns and seven eyes, which are the seven Spirits of God sent out into all the earth.
⁷ Then He came and took the scroll out of the right hand of Him who sat on the throne.

Jesus is standing before God's throne, the four living creatures, and the elders. He looks like a Lamb that had just been slain and has seven horns and seven eyes, which are the seven Spirits of God, then He comes and takes the scroll out of the right hand of God. I believe that Jesus looking like a Lamb that had just been slain taking the scroll from God's right hand to begin releasing its seals is a clue as to when these seals began to be released. This is the only vison Jesus is seen as a Lamb that had just been slain. I believe God let John see it this way because it was literally the way it happened, and so the reader could understand when this began, that when Jesus had just recently been crucified on the earth as the Lamb of God, He is now in heaven standing before the throne of God, His Father, and the four living creatures and the elders as the only one in heaven and earth and under the earth worthy to take the scroll out of God's right hand and release its seals and open it.

WORTHY IS THE LAMB

The rest of *Revelation 5* describes what happens after the Lamb takes the scroll out of the right hand of God. The living creatures and the elders fall down, and hundreds of millions and millions of millions of angels sing a new song and worship the Lamb.

THE FIRST SEAL

REVELATION 6:1-2 (NKJV)
¹ Then I saw when the Lamb broke one of the seven seals, and I heard one of the four living creatures saying as with a voice of thunder, "Come!"
² I looked, and behold, a white horse, and the one who sat on it had a bow; and a crown was given to him, and he went out conquering and to conquer.

The Lamb breaks the First Seal, and one of the four living creatures says to John with a voice like thunder, "Come!" and John looks and sees a white horse and rider, who has a bow and is given a crown, that he goes out conquering to conquer. Who is this rider on the white horse? This verse does not reveal the identity of the rider on the white horse, but the Lord Jesus Christ also comes back riding a white horse. Let's take a close look at the Scriptures that describe Christ coming back on a white horse and then compare them to this passage.

REVELATION 19:11-16 (NKJV)
¹¹ And I saw heaven opened, and behold, a white horse, and He who sat on it is called Faithful and True, and in righteousness He judges and wages war.
¹² His eyes are a flame of fire, and on His head are many crowns; and He has a name written on Him which no one knows except Himself.
¹³ He is clothed with a robe dipped in blood, and His name is called The Word of God.
¹⁴ And the armies which are in heaven, clothed in fine linen,

white and clean, were following Him on white horses.

[15] From His mouth comes a sharp sword, so that with it He may strike down the nations, and He will rule them with a rod of iron; and He treads the wine press of the fierce wrath of God, the Almighty.

[16] And on His robe and on His thigh He has a name written: "KING OF KINGS, AND LORD OF LORDS."

The first thing you notice is that heaven is opened, and this white horse is in heaven. Next, the verse gives a very detailed description of the rider; He is Faithful and True, He judges and wages war in righteousness, His eyes are a flame of fire, He is wearing many crowns and has a name no one knows except Him, He is clothed with a robe dipped in blood and His name is The Word of God. A sharp sword comes from His mouth that strikes down the nations and He will rule them with an iron rod. He treads the winepress of the wrath of God, and on His robe and on His thigh, He has a name written, *"King of kings and Lord of lords."*

We will compare this white horse rider, who we know is the Lord Jesus Christ, to the rider on the white horse seen by John after the First Seal is broken. The white horse and rider who is identified as the Lord Jesus Christ is clearly coming from heaven because John says he saw heaven opened, and when he sees the white horse and rider after the First Seal is broken, there is no indication that the white horse and rider comes from heaven. The reason we know the white horse and rider in *Revelation 19* is the Lord Jesus Christ is because He is identified three times, He is Faithful and True, His name is the Word of God. It is written two places, on His robe and on His thigh that He is the King of kings and Lord of lords. Yet, there is absolutely no identification of who the rider is on the white horse seen after the First Seal is released. The Lord Jesus Christ is wearing many crowns and the rider seen in the vision of the First Seal is wearing only one crown. The Lord is coming back to judge and make war in righteousness and uses the sword of His mouth, and the rider seen in the vision of the First Seal has a bow and is going out to conquer, and it says nothing about conquering with righteousness. A complete list of attributes about these two riders in comparison will make it easier to identify the similarities and differences.

A list of attributes of the two riders for comparison:

RIDER IN REVELATION 6	RIDER IN REVELATION 19
Rider is seen in the vision of the First Seal	Rider is the Lord Jesus Christ
Riding on a white horse	Riding on a white horse
No indication of coming from heaven	Comes from heaven
Does not reveal who the rider is	Identified three times as the Lord Jesus Christ
Given one crown	Given many crowns
Goes out to conquer, does not reveal the purpose	Judges and makes war in righteousness
Weapon: A bow, no mention of arrows	Weapon: A sword from his mouth
No description of what the rider is wearing	Dressed in a robe dipped in blood with his name written on his thigh
No description of the rider's eyes	His eyes are a flame of fire
No description of anyone following	Armies of heaven followed Him, clothed in white robes

From this list comparing these two riders, the only thing truly the same about these two riders is that they are both riding white horses. Everything else is different enough to indicate that these riders are not the same person. Another important fact is that the Lord is in heaven during the vision of the rider on the white horse in the First Seal, and we know the Lord Jesus Christ is seated at the right a hand of God, His Father, until He returns. So, if the rider on the white horse seen in the vision of the First Seal is not Christ, who is he? The fact that he has some similarities to Christ in that he is riding a white horse and has a crown appearing to be a king or ruler could mean that this rider is intended to appear to be Christ but is not. That would mean the rider is a false christ. In Jesus' warnings about the signs before the end and the Tribulation in *Matthew 24:4* and *Mark 13:6*, the first thing He said was many false christs would come. The fact that Jesus said there would be many false christs indicates the false christs are a spirit and not just a person. The Apostle John called them antichrists. Let's read what he has to say about that.

1 JOHN 2:18 (NKJV)

[18] Little children, it is the last hour; and as you have heard that the Antichrist is coming, even now many antichrists

have come, by which we know that it is the last hour.

The Apostle John says, *"you have heard the Antichrist is coming."* Singular. We know at the very end that there will be a single antichrist who is the beast in *Revelation* and the man of sin and son of perdition revealed by the Apostle Paul. Then John says many antichrists have already come, confirming there is an antichrist spirit that is moving in the earth and spreading. This would indicate the rider on the white horse is a spirit, and the horse represents the ability to cover more ground and move faster. A finite spirit cannot cover the earth instantly but has to spread its influence over time, but the horse, allowing faster movement, would allow the rider to spread its influence faster. John saying that there were already many antichrists in the early Church suggests the spirit was spreading its influence fast and early. We know from 2 *Thessalonians* 2 that the Lord is holding back this spirit from taking over the world, until He removes His Spirit, then this spirit will be able to quickly finish spreading and taking over the world except for those who truly belong to Christ. Since the Scripture does not say exactly who this rider on the white horse is, and only gives the clues we just covered, we cannot with one-hundred percent certainty identify who this rider on the white horse is, seen in the vision by John when the First Seal is released. Knowing with some certainty, he is not Christ, all the clues point to it being the spirit of antichrist. I think we can conclude with some certainty that the rider on the white horse who John saw in the vision of the First Seal is the spirit of the antichrist.

THE SECOND SEAL

REVELATION 6:3-4 (NKJV)
3 When He opened the Second Seal, I heard the second living creature saying, "Come and see."
4 Another horse, fiery red, went out. And it was granted to the one who sat on it to take peace from the earth, and that people should kill one another; and there was given to him a great sword.

When the Second Seal is released, John is given a vision of a fiery red horse and its rider is granted to take peace from the earth and cause people to kill one another, and he was given a great sword. Again, the rider is not identified, but he is granted to take peace from the earth and cause people to kill one another. Just like the first horse and rider, no finite spirit can cause its influence to spread across the entire earth instantaneously. The horse providing increased speed and movement would cause it to spread faster, but still the spread of violence and war will be a progressive increase over time. Comparing the second horse and rider to the Lord's warning of signs before the Tribulation and the end, the Lord said the second type of events that will occur will be wars and rumors wars. Nation will rise against nation and kingdom against kingdom, indicating an increase in war and violence, just like the rider on the fiery red horse is going to cause.

THE THIRD SEAL

REVELATION 6:5-6 (NKJV)
⁵ When He opened the Third Seal, I heard the third living creature say, "Come and see." So I looked, and behold, a black horse, and he who sat on it had a pair of scales in his hand.
⁶ And I heard a voice in the midst of the four living creatures saying, "A quart of wheat for a denarius, and three quarts of barley for a denarius; and do not harm the oil and the wine."

When the Third Seal is released, the third creature says to John *"Come and see,"* and John is given a vision of a black horse and its rider had a pair of scales in his hand. A voice from the four creatures said, *"a quart of wheat for a denarius."* A quart of wheat is about enough wheat for a large loaf of bread, which is enough to feed one person for a day, and a denarius was a day's wages, so a quart of wheat for a denarius meant it costs a full day's wages to feed one person. Food costing that much can only mean one thing—Severe famine. The third thing Jesus said would increase before the Tribulation and end was famine.

THE FOURTH SEAL

REVELATION 6:7-8 (NKJV)
7 When He opened the Fourth Seal, I heard the voice of the fourth living creature saying, "Come and see."
8 So I looked, and behold, a pale horse. And the name of him who sat on it was Death, and Hades followed with him. And power was given to them over a fourth of the earth, to kill with sword, with hunger, with death, and by the beasts of the earth.

When the Fourth Seal is released, the fourth creature says to John *"Come and see,"* and John is given a vision of a pale horse and its rider's name is Death and hell follows him. This is the first rider who has been identified, and his name is Death and hell is following him. If hell is following Death on the earth, it means death and a horde of evil spirits from hell have been released on the earth. Power was given to them over twenty-five percent of the earth to kill with the sword, hunger, death (pestilence), and the beasts of the earth. The word "death" here is also translated to pestilence and by the beast of the earth. Death and its horde from hell are given power over a fourth of the earth to kill, though it does not say that they killed a fourth of the earth but that they have power over a fourth of the earth to kill with sword, famine, death (pestilence), and the beasts of the earth.

Now this fourth horse and rider kills with the sword and famine, the same as the second and third horses and riders, but the fourth horse and rider also kills with death (pestilence) and the beasts of the earth. Pestilence is the fourth thing Jesus said in *Matthew 24* that would increase on the earth before the Tribulation and the end. Considering the clues given, when the first horse and rider, who is presumably the antichrist, was released, Christ is seen as a Lamb who had just been slain, not sitting at the right-hand of His Father. The second clue is the Apostle John revealed that antichrists were already on the earth during the time of his ministry, and that would have been after the life, death, and Resurrection of Christ. With this, we can estimate that the first horse and rider was released on the earth sometime soon after the death of Christ. These horses and riders are finite spirits who cannot spread their influence instantaneously on the earth but would have to spread

it progressively over time and would likely be experiencing some resistance from the saints, slowing their progression some. The warnings Jesus gave of the antichrists, war, famine, and pestilence increasing on earth before the Tribulation and the end, these are the exact same things released on the earth by the four horses and riders in the exact same order. Using the limited clues provided by Scripture to estimate when these horses and riders may have been released, the first horse and rider appears to be released soon after the death and crucifixion of Christ, and all four before the Tribulation, causing what Jesus called the beginning of sorrows, or birth pains, which continue to increase until they give birth to the Tribulation. All four of these horses and riders could have been released soon after the death of Christ, or any time after the death Christ, until sometime before the Tribulation. Early enough to increase to the levels that Jesus indicated they would before the Tribulation. The final take we get from this is summed up in what Jesus said, there would be antichrists, a significant increase in war, famine, pestilence, and earthquakes in various places before the Tribulation. As we see these things increase to levels never seen or heard of before, and are continuing to increase, we know the time of the Tribulation is getting close.

THE FIFTH SEAL

REVELATION 6:9-11 (NKJV)
9 When He opened the Fifth Seal, I saw under the altar the souls of those who had been slain for the word of God and for the testimony which they held.
10 And they cried with a loud voice, saying, "How long, O Lord, holy and true, until You judge and avenge our blood on those who dwell on the earth?"
11 Then a white robe was given to each of them; and it was said to them that they should rest a little while longer, until both the number of their fellow servants and their brethren, who would be killed as they were, was completed.

Notice John is now seeing a vision in heaven, and no one is telling him to come and see as they did during the visions of the first four seals. John sees the saints that have been martyred through the ages under

the alter asking the Lord how long until He judges and avenges their blood on those on the earth who have killed them. White robes are given to them, and they are told to wait a little while longer until the rest of the saints are martyred as they were. There are two clues here as to possibly when the vision of this seal occurs—First, the martyrs of the ages are asking the Lord when their blood will be avenged, and they are already in heaven and may know that the time is near. Second, they are given white robes, the same thing the saints are wearing when they follow the Lord back to the earth at His coming. Third, they are told to wait just a little longer until the rest of the saints that are to be martyred are killed, and that would include the Tribulation saints. With these three clues, we can estimate this vision occurs sometime soon before the Great Tribulation.

THE SIXTH SEAL

REVELATION 6:12-13 (NKJV)
[12] I looked when He opened the Sixth Seal, and behold, there was a great earthquake; and the sun became black as sackcloth of hair, and the moon became like blood.
[13] And the stars of heaven fell to the earth, as a fig tree drops its late figs when it is shaken by a mighty wind.

When the Sixth Seal is released, John sees a vision of a great earthquake. The sun turns black, the moon turns blood red, and stars fall from heaven to the earth. These are the same events Jesus taught would happen after the Tribulation and right before His coming in the sky to Rapture and resurrect the saints. Let's compare the two passages.

MATTHEW 24:29 (NKJV)
[29] "Immediately after the tribulation of those days the sun will be darkened, and the moon will not give its light; the stars will fall from heaven, and the powers of the heavens will be shaken.

Jesus says the sun will be darkened and John says the sun will turn black. The Lord says the stars will fall from heaven and the powers of the heavens will be shaken, and John says the stars fall from heaven to the earth like a fig tree shaken by a mighty wind. Jesus says the moon does not give its light, but does not say the moon cannot be seen, and John says the moon was blood red or dark red. The moon was created to be a night light to the earth. The moon's natural color is between a soft white and a light yellow, and when it is these colors, it is a good night light to the earth. A blood red or dark red moon would be visible but would not provide a bright enough light to be a usable night light to the earth. From our analysis of the first few verses of both passages, we can see that these are very likely the same event, and as we continue to study the rest of these passages, we will see that they are definitely the same event.

REVELATION 6:14-17 (NKJV)

14 Then the sky receded as a scroll when it is rolled up, and every mountain and island was moved out of its place.
15 And the kings of the earth, the great men, the rich men, the commanders, the mighty men, every slave and every free man, hid themselves in the caves and in the rocks of the mountains,
16 and said to the mountains and rocks, "Fall on us and hide us from the face of Him who sits on the throne and from the wrath of the Lamb!
17 For the great day of His wrath has come, and who is able to stand?"

John sees the sky rolled back like a scroll. From the greatest to the least, they try and hide themselves in caves, rocks, and mountains, and they want the mountains and rocks to fall on them and hide them from the face of Him who sits on the throne and the wrath of the Lamb. If they are so desperate to hide themselves from the face of God and the wrath of the Lamb that they want the mountains and rocks to fall on them, then they must really be seeing Almighty God on His throne and the coming of Christ. The sky receding like a scroll really means that the veil between heaven and earth has opened and they can see God and Christ, and that agrees with what Jesus said when He comes. Everyone will see Him!

MATTHEW 24:30 (NKJV)

30 Then the sign of the Son of Man will appear in heaven, and then all the tribes of the earth will mourn, and they will see the Son of Man coming on the clouds of heaven

with power and great glory.

The Lord says all the tribes of the earth will cry when they see Him coming from heaven with power and great glory. The two passages together complete this picture. Many people will know they are going to receive God's wrath and they are going to try desperately to hide themselves. Many are going to cry because they know God's wrath is coming and that there truly is no escape, and many will cry because they knew to be ready and to prepare for His coming, but they did not, and now they are going to receive His wrath. Revelation 11 is another passage that reveals the coming of Christ, the Resurrection, and His wrath to come.

REVELATION 11:15,18 (NKJV)

15 Then the seventh angel sounded: And there were loud voices in heaven, saying, "The kingdoms of this world have become the kingdoms of our Lord and of His Christ, and He shall reign forever and ever!"
18 The nations were angry, and Your wrath has come, And the time of the dead, that they should be judged, And that You should reward Your servants the prophets and the saints, And those who fear Your name, small and great, And should destroy those who destroy the earth."

The Seventh and Last Trumpet of God is sounded, a declaration is made stating the kingdoms of this world have become the kingdoms of God and Christ. The nations are angry because there has been great trouble on the earth. God's wrath has come with the time of judging and rewarding His servants, the prophets and the saints and all those who fear His name, small and great. This is the first Resurrection. Jesus called it the Resurrection of the Just, and it will include the Rapture since the Rapture is part of the first Resurrection. This is the same thing John saw in the vision of the Sixth Seal being released, God's wrath has come, and Christ is coming to execute His wrath after He judges and rewards all His servants. Let's continue comparing this with what Jesus says.

MATTHEW 24:31 (NKJV)

31 And He will send His angels with a great sound of a trumpet, and they will gather together His elect from the

four winds, from one end of heaven to the other.

MARK 13:27 (NKJV)
²⁷ And then He will send His angels, and gather together His elect from the four winds, from the farthest part of earth to the farthest part of heaven.

The Trumpet of God is sounded by an angel in heaven and the Lord sends His angels to gather His people from the farthest parts of the earth. This is the Rapture of those still alive on the earth. From the farthest parts of heaven are the saints coming back with Him who will be in the Resurrection and receive their glorified bodies. Now that we have compared the Scriptures of the vision John sees at the release of the Sixth Seal and the coming of Christ after the Tribulation in the Gospels, and the sounding of the Seventh Trumpet in *Revelation 11*, let's look at a summary of them.

1. The Sixth Seal and Jesus both reveal the same events just prior to the coming of Christ, and they are: The sun is dark, the moon does not give its light, and the stars fall from heaven.
2. The Sixth Seal and Jesus both reveal that Christ is seen by the entire earth when He comes.
3. The Sixth Seal and the Seventh Trumpet both declare God's wrath to the whole world has come.
4. The Sixth Seal says people will desperately try to hide from God's wrath when they see Christ coming. Jesus says people will be crying when they see Christ coming.
5. The Seventh Trumpet and Jesus both reveal that the sounding of the Last Trumpet of God will be the coming of Christ, the Resurrection, the Rapture, and judgement to reward God's servants.

Final conclusion—The Sixth Seal, the Seventh Trumpet, and the coming of Christ are all the same event.

This brings up an interesting situation, since we learned in a previous chapter that the Seven Trumpets are not revealed until the Seventh Seal is broken allowing the scroll to be opened and reveal the Seven Trumpets, how can the Sixth Seal be a vision of the Seventh

Trumpet since the Seven Trumpets are not revealed until the Seventh Seal is released? I believe the answer is that the Seven Seals are just visions and not actual judgements being released, unlike the case with the Seven Trumpets being sounded. Let me explain, when John sees Christ open the seals, He is seen as Lamb that had just been slain, and this is the only time in Scripture that He is seen this way. It gives us a sign that Christ opened, or started to open, these seals soon after His crucifixion where He was the Lamb that had just been slain. The visions of the first four seals are events on the earth and are the same events in the same order as the birth pains that Jesus describes taking place before the Tribulation. We know from the Scripture in *1 John 2:18* that the spirit of the antichrist was on the earth soon after Christ's death, and the other three plagues released on the earth by the other three horsemen; war, feminine, and death, will take time to build up to the level they will be at right before the Tribulation. There is no way to know for sure if they were actually released soon after Christ's death or closer to the time of the Tribulation, but on the other hand, since they become the birth pains that lead up to the Tribulation, it is possible the events, not the vision seen at the release of the seals, are closer to the time of the Tribulation. The Fifth Seal is a vison in heaven of the martyrs under the alter asking God when their blood will be avenged, and they are told to wait a little while longer until all the martyrs, including those of the Great Tribulation, are complete. This gives us a sign that this event, not the vision of Fifth Seal, may be close to the time of the Great Tribulation. The Fifth Seal is clearly just a vision and not a judgement of God, as seen in the vision of the first four seals, and the Sixth Seal is a vision of the coming of Christ at the end of the Tribulation and the Seventh Trumpet. If the First Seal's horse and rider is indeed the spirit of the antichrist, which the spirit of the antichrist was definitely present soon after the death of Christ as John says in *1 John 2:18*, and the Sixth Seal is a vision of the coming of Christ, then the release of the first six seals are just visions of what happens between the time that Christ was on the earth the first time until the coming of Christ the second time at the Last Trumpet. Since the only clue as to when the seals were released was Jesus appearing as a Lamb that had just been slain, which is the only time He appears this way, and the seals are visions, many of them being far in the future, it is possible these seals were released soon after Christ's crucifixion, and John was seeing visions of the future at the release of each seal. Since the event of the Sixth Seal is the coming of

Christ at the Seventh Trumpet, the seals are visions of events, and future events, and not the release of judgements that occur at the sounding of the Seven Trumpets. Next, in *Revelation 7*, John sees another vision.

REVELATION 7:1-4 (NKJV)

1 After these things I saw four angels standing at the four corners of the earth, holding the four winds of the earth, that the wind should not blow on the earth, on the sea, or on any tree.

2 Then I saw another angel ascending from the east, having the seal of the living God. And he cried with a loud voice to the four angels to whom it was granted to harm the earth and the sea,

3 saying, "Do not harm the earth, the sea, or the trees till we have sealed the servants of our God on their foreheads."

4 And I heard the number of those who were sealed. One hundred and forty-four thousand of all the tribes of the children of Israel were sealed:

Verses 5-8 describe twelve thousand who are sealed from each of the twelve tribes of Israel; Judah, Reuben, Gad, Asher, Naphtali, Manasseh, Simeon, Levi, Issachar, Zebulun, Joseph, and Benjamin, equaling one-hundred and forty-four thousand that are sealed. John sees a vision of four angels holding back the four winds, and these same four angels have been given power to harm the earth and the sea. Then he sees an angel telling them not to harm the earth, the sea, or the trees until the one-hundred and forty-four thousand are sealed. The four angels are told to hold back these judgements of God until the one-hundred and forty-four thousand are sealed because the judgments of God are not against His saints but against the wicked. These are sealed to God before these judgements come on the earth, the sea, and the trees so that they can be identified as belonging to God and not be harmed by these judgements. Next, in *Revelation 7:9-16*, John sees a vision of a great multitude that no one could number from all the nations that have come out of the Great Tribulation. They are clothed in white robes, washed by the blood of the Lamb, standing before God and Christ worshiping Them. They will serve God before His throne and He will dwell with them, and Christ will shepherd them and lead them

to fountains of living waters, and they will never suffer, hunger, or thirst ever again, and God will wipe away all their tears.

THE SEVENTH SEAL

One important point to make about the Seventh Seal before we study it; the Seventh Seal is the last seal on the scroll, therefore allowing the scroll to be opened and reveal what is inside.

REVELATION 8:1 (NKJV)
¹ When He opened the Seventh Seal, there was silence in heaven for about half an hour.

Verse 1 says there was silence in heaven for about half an hour. The half hour of silence is in heaven so that the measure of time would be based on heaven's timeclock, not the earth's. So, what is heaven's timeclock? I believe the following Scriptures will help us understand that.

PSALM 90:4 (NKJV)
⁴ For a thousand years in Your sight Are like yesterday when it is past, And like a watch in the night.

2 PETER 3:8 (NKJV)
⁸ But, beloved, do not forget this one thing, that with the Lord one day is as a thousand years, and a thousand years as one day.

These Scriptures say one day is a thousand years with the Lord. The Lord is in heaven, so I believe these Scriptures are saying heaven's time is one day for every thousand years on the earth. If you do the math of converting one-thousand earth years to one day in heaven, half an hour in heaven would be approximately 20.8 years on the earth. *Revelation 8:1* says about half an hour, so heaven is waiting approximately twenty years before continuing with what is revealed inside the scroll after the Seventh and Last Seal is broken, allowing the scroll to be opened. Continuing with the next verses in *Revelation 8:2-6.*

REVELATION 8:2 (NKJV)
² And I saw the seven angels who stand before God, and to them were given seven trumpets.

The first thing John sees after the scroll has been opened, and after the half hour in heaven has passed, are seven angels who are given Seven Trumpets.

REVELATION 8:3-5 (NKJV)
³ Then another angel, having a golden censer, came and stood at the altar. He was given much incense, that he should offer it with the prayers of all the saints upon the golden altar which was before the throne.
⁴ And the smoke of the incense, with the prayers of the saints, ascended before God from the angel's hand.
⁵ Then the angel took the censer, filled it with fire from the altar, and threw it to the earth. And there were noises, thundering's, lightnings, and an earthquake.

John sees another angel with a golden censer who came and stood at the altar. The angel is given a lot of incense to offer with the prayers of the saints on the golden altar in front of the throne, and the smoke from the incense and prayers of the saints went up from the angel's hand to God. The angel filled the censer with fire from the altar and threw it to the earth, causing noises, thundering, lightning, and an earthquake.

REVELATION 8:6 (NKJV)
⁶ So the seven angels who had the seven trumpets prepared themselves to sound.

John sees the seven angels with the Seven Trumpets prepared to sound them. Previously we learned that the Seventh and Last Trumpet is the Resurrection and Rapture of the saints. We learned some things about the Sixth Trumpet, including the three-and-a-half-year, or forty-two-month, rein of the beast who makes war with the saints, which occurs, or at least most of it, during the timeframe of the Sixth Trumpet. Now having learned what events lead up to the Tribulation; antichrists, war, famine, and death gaining control of one-fourth of the world's

population, and with power to kill with war, famine, pestilence, and wild beasts, it is time to look at all the Trumpet Judgements from the First Trumpet to the Last Trumpet to better understand the events that will lead up to the Rapture and Resurrection.

THE FIRST TRUMPET

REVELATION 8:7 (NKJV)
7 The first angel sounded: And hail and fire followed, mingled with blood, and they were thrown to the earth. And a third of the trees were burned up, and all green grass was burned up.

The First Trumpet releases hail and fire mingled with blood, and it burns up a third of the earth and trees and all the green grass. This is a serious judgment of God and leads to a question; Are there other judgments in Scripture that are like this one? The answer is yes, there are, they are in *Exodus 9:18-29*. The Lord sends down hail mixed with fire and destroys man, beast, trees, and vegetation in all the land of Egypt, except nearby in Goshen where God's people lived where there was no hail. This similar judgement in Egypt shows that God can and does bring judgement on the wicked and protects His people from these judgements.

THE SECOND TRUMPET

REVELATION 8:8-9 (NKJV)
8 Then the second angel sounded: And something like a great mountain burning with fire was thrown into the sea, and a third of the sea became blood.
9 And a third of the living creatures in the sea died, and a third of the ships were destroyed.

This Second Trumpet judgment sounds like a huge blazing asteroid, and since John would probably not know what an asteroid is, a huge blazing mountain would most likely be the way he would have described a huge blazing mountain size asteroid. There's no doubt God could throw a huge blazing mountain into the sea, but in either case, a huge blazing mountain sized object is thrown into the sea. I don't think

we are going to find anything like that, that has ever occurred before in the Bible. So, is there anything the Bible can tell us about this? For one thing, since nothing like this blazing mountain or asteroid has ever happened before, we can be certain this judgment has not happened yet. In fact, nothing on the scale of this judgement, a semi-global event of one third of the earth suffering devastation, has happened since Noah's flood, which was a full global judgment. There's one part of this judgment that does have something in common with an earlier Bible event, and that is the sea turning to blood and everything in the sea dying. That is when the Lord in His judgment of Egypt in a series of plagues that were the same series of judgements the plague of hail and fire just mentioned are part of. The Lord turned the Nile into blood and all the fish in the Nile died. This is found *Exodus 7:14-21*.

THE THIRD TRUMPET

REVELATION 8:10-11 (NKJV)
[10] Then the third angel sounded: And a great star fell from heaven, burning like a torch, and it fell on a third of the rivers and on the springs of water.
[11] The name of the star is Wormwood. A third of the waters became wormwood, and many men died from the water, because it was made bitter.

A great star falling from heaven definitely sounds like an Asteroid, and the fact that it immediately follows the first blazing asteroid gives the possibility that this second asteroid could be another part of the first asteroid if it were to break up at some point. There is also another possibility that comes to mind, this second asteroid or second part of the first asteroid could possibly break up into many pieces striking many of the fresh water sources of the earth with its poison. Regardless of exactly how this burning poisonous object named *wormwood* strikes the earth, the result of this judgment is a third of the earth's fresh waters being poisoned causing in many deaths. Since this is a judgement of God, and the Bible has a long history of God protecting His holy people who trust and obey Him from His punishment of the wicked, I believe those who walk wholeheartedly in faith and obedience to God will very likely be protected from these judgements since these trumpet judgements are against the wicked and

not against God's holy people.

THE FOURTH TRUMPET

REVELATION 8:12 (NKJV)

¹² Then the fourth angel sounded: And a third of the sun was struck, a third of the moon, and a third of the stars, so that a third of them were darkened. A third of the day did not shine, and likewise the night

Again, this Trumpet Judgement affects one third of the earth, and this time it is the earth's natural lights, sunlight, moonlight, and starlight. Question—Are there any other judgements similar to this one in Scripture to compare and help understand this one? Yes, there is, as we have seen with the previous Trumpet Judgements, they are similar to the judgments against Egypt. When God delivered the Israelites from the harsh slavery of Egypt, the scale of those judgements were different. The judgements against Egypt were on a national scale and the Trumpet Judgements are on a semi-global scale of one third of the earth. In *Exodus 10*, God covered the whole land of Egypt with thick darkness, so dark that nobody could move around, yet God's people had light where they lived. Again, this should encourage us that God can and does protect His saints from His Judgments. The entire account of this plague against Egypt is found in *Exodus 10:21-23*.

THE THREE WOES

REVELATION 8:13 (NKJV)

¹³ And I looked, and I heard an angel flying through the midst of heaven, saying with a loud voice, "Woe, woe, woe to the inhabitants of the earth, because of the remaining blasts of the trumpet of the three angels who are about to sound!"

The next three Trumpet Judgements are declared as Three Woes. Not once, but three times, indicating these are going to be very severe and terrible judgments.

THE FIFTH TRUMPET

REVELATION 9:1-2 (NKJV)
¹ Then the fifth angel sounded: And I saw a star fallen from heaven to the earth. To him was given the key to the bottomless pit.
² And he opened the bottomless pit, and smoke arose out of the pit like the smoke of a great furnace. So the sun and the air were darkened because of the smoke of the pit.

Stars in the Bible are often symbolic representations of angels, since this star is *a him*, indicating a personage, and later in this passage it actually reveals it is an angel, and since he fell from heaven we know that he is a fallen angel. There is more detail about this fallen angel later in this passage, including his name in *Revelation 9:11*. The fallen angel is given a key to the bottomless pit and uses the key to open the bottomless pit, also called the abyss. It says smoke rises out of this bottomless pit like a great furnace.

2 PETER 2:4 (NKJV)
⁴ For if God spared not the angels that sinned, but cast them down to hell, and delivered them into chains of darkness, to be reserved unto judgment;

2 Peter 2:4 reveals that hell is a prison for fallen angels, which the devil and his demons are all fallen angels.

MARK 9:43 (NKJV)
⁴³ If your hand causes you to sin, cut it off. It is better for you to enter into life maimed, rather than having two hands, to go to hell, into the fire that shall never be quenched—

Mark 9:43 says hell is a place of fire and torment that will never be quenched. *Revelation 9:1* says smoke rises out of the bottomless pit like a great furnace, so the bottomless pit is a great furnace of fire.

REVELATION 20:1-3,7 (NKJV)
¹ Then I saw an angel coming down from heaven, having the key to the bottomless pit and a great chain in his hand.

² He laid hold of the dragon, that serpent of old, who is the Devil and Satan, and bound him for a thousand years;
³ and he cast him into the bottomless pit, and shut him up, and set a seal on him, so that he should deceive the nations no more till the thousand years were finished. But after these things he must be released for a little while.
⁷ Now when the thousand years have expired, Satan will be released from his prison

Revelation 20:1-3,7 says Satan is thrown into the abyss as his prison for one-thousand years, the abyss being a fiery furnace. Hell is place of fire and a prison for fallen angels, and the devil and his demons are fallen angels. As you can see, Scripture reveals the bottomless pit, the abyss, is located in and is a part of hell. With that understanding, we will be able to better understand the Fifth Trumpet Judgement.

REVELATION 9:3-4 (NKJV)
³ Then out of the smoke locusts came upon the earth. And to them was given power, as the scorpions of the earth have power.
⁴ They were commanded not to harm the grass of the earth, or any green thing, or any tree, but only those men who do not have the seal of God on their foreheads.

These locust creatures come up, and on, the earth out of the smoke of the bottomless pit that is in hell. That means these locusts are coming up out of hell. We know hell is a prison for the devil and his demons, and since these creatures are coming up out of hell, we know they are some kind of demonic creature. They are told not to hurt the vegetation or the trees, the things locusts would normally harm, but only the people who don't have the seal of God on their forehead. Scripture says all true believers are sealed by the Holy Spirit.

EPHESIANS 1:13 (NKJV)
¹³ In Him you also trusted, after you heard the word of truth, the Gospel of your salvation; in whom also, having believed, you were sealed with the Holy Spirit of promise,

In *Revelation 7:1-8,* the one-hundred-forty-four thousand are sealed as firstfruits to God and Christ from all the twelve tribes of Israel.

Scripture shows they are sealed before the Trumpet Judgments so they will not suffer the punishment of the Fifth Trumpet Judgment, or any of the other Trumpet Judgements. The Lord is making a distinction here between His people and the sinful people of the world just like He did with the judgements of Egypt, Sodom and Gomorrah, and Noah's flood. There is no mention of the mark of the beast, only those who do not have the seal of God. Remember from chapter seven; *When is the Rapture?* The mark of the beast is not implemented until sometime after the sounding of the Sixth Trumpet and during the three-and-a-half-year global reign of the beast. So, no one would have the mark of the beast during the Fifth Trumpet.

REVELATION 9:5-6 (NKJV)

⁵ And they were not given authority to kill them, but to torment them for five months. Their torment was like the torment of a scorpion when it strikes a man.
⁶ In those days' men will seek death and will not find it; they will desire to die, and death will flee from them.

The torment these demonic locust-like creatures inflict is going to be so severe people are going to want to die from it, and Scripture says they won't be able to die. They will seek death, but it will flee from them. Seeking death usually means attempting suicide, except in this case they will not be able to kill themselves because death is going to flee from them. It does not say they will not suffer, so those who breaks bones or do other bodily harm to themselves will increase their own suffering with the injuries they inflict on themselves. Think about this; with everyone who is not a truly sealed believer in Christ, which will be a majority of the human race at this point, it is very possible the world is going to notice that the saints are not suffering from this plague and will persecute them for it. It says that this torment will be for five months, verse 10 repeats the fact that this will be for five months, so why would the Lord repeat this time period twice? I believe it is because He wants His people to know that this Fifth Trumpet Judgement will only last for five months. This leads to another question—Why would God want us to know that this judgement is only going last for five months? Remember, the Fifth Trumpet is the first of Three Woes, and these judgments are getting worse, and though His people may be spared these judgements, it is very likely global persecution is

increasing. I believe He is beginning to give His people the length of time of these judgements so they can begin to understand how close the end is. Maybe not the day or hour, but possibly the year or month since the Rapture is at the sounding of the Seventh Trumpet. We know this Fifth Trumpet is only five months, and we learned when we studied some of the Sixth Trumpet that it is at least three-and-a-half-years, which is forty-two months or one-thousand-two-hundred-and-sixty days, but it is actually a little longer than three-and-a-half-years, which we will soon learn as we study the rest of the events of the Sixth Trumpet. In *Daniel 12*, it says the wise will understand, so the saints will understand that the end is approaching. This will help them keep their eyes on the Lord Jesus and eternity and not their lives in this world.

THE SIXTH TRUMPET

REVELATION 9:13-16 (NKJV)
13 Then the sixth angel sounded: And I heard a voice from the four horns of the golden altar which is before God,
14 saying to the sixth angel who had the trumpet, "Release the four angels who are bound at the great river Euphrates."
15 So the four angels, who had been prepared for the hour and day and month and year, were released to kill a third of mankind.
16 Now the number of the army of the horsemen was two hundred million; I heard the number of them.

These four angels who have been bound, will, with an of army of two-hundred million, kill a third of mankind. The next section of this passage describes the army of two-hundred million horsemen. *Revelation 9:17* gives a vivid description of this army. The passage gives no indication that this army is from hell like the demonic locusts, only that it is used by the four angels who were bound in the Euphrates River. With that, I believe this army is a human army, beyond that I do not fully understand what this army is, and for the purposes of this study, we will focus on what Scriptures says is the result of this army's campaign, and that is, it kills a third of mankind.

One thing of interest is the statement that they were prepared for

the hour and day and month and year, with a year being the longest period of time mentioned and all other times can be contained in that year. Could this be saying this war will only last one year or even less? An army of two-hundred million is bigger than all the armies in the world combined at this present time. With an army of that size, it could be possible to kill a third of mankind in a year. The next passages describe the condition of the rest of mankind. We know from studying later events of the Sixth Trumpet that the beast rules all the nations for three-and-a-half-years, and he was at the beginning of his global reign being praised and worshiped for being healed of a mortal wound with the saying *"who can make war with the beast?"* indicating he was a great warrior and conqueror since this war occurred just before his global reign. It is likely that this is the war that led him to global power, and in fact, the book of the Prophet Daniel also mentions the beast being in war leading up to his final reign. The book of Daniel also says his rein is three-and-a-half-years, which is the exact same length of time as the forty-two months that the book of *Revelation* reveals will be the length of his global rein.

REVELATION 9:20-21 (NKJV)
20 But the rest of mankind, who were not killed by these plagues, did not repent of the works of their hands, that they should not worship demons, and idols of gold, silver, brass, stone, and wood, which can neither see nor hear nor walk.
21 And they did not repent of their murders or their sorceries or their sexual immorality or their thefts.

Instead of fearing God and repenting, they continue in their wickedness. They are probably afraid of what is happening on the earth, but their hearts are so hard they seem to be unable to repent. They are responding to God's Judgements in a similar way to Pharaoh in Egypt in *Exodus 9:12*. We should take this as a serious warning and realize the time of repentance may be over when these judgements come.

REVELATION 11:13-14 (NKJV)
13 In the same hour there was a great earthquake, and a tenth of the city fell. In the earthquake seven thousand people were killed, and the rest were afraid and gave glory to the God of heaven.

¹⁴ The second woe is past. Behold, the third woe is coming quickly.

The last event of the Sixth Trumpet is a great earthquake that causes a tenth of the city to fall and seven thousand people in the city to be killed. I believe that this city is Jerusalem because this earthquake follows the two witnesses being raised to life and called up to heaven, which the two witnesses were prophesying from Jerusalem. We see the rest of the people of the city are afraid and gave glory to God, the exact opposite to the response from the rest world, who after all the previous plagues, and a world war that kills a third of mankind, do not repent and certainly do not glorify God. How can this be? On one hand, the entire gentile world does not repent of their wicked deeds or glorify God after receiving severe judgements and global war, and on the other hand, we see what looks like repentance in the city of Jerusalem after this great earthquake.

This is what I believe is happening, Scripture teaches the time of the gentiles will come to an end in *Luke 21:24*, the Gospel has been preached to the gentile world for over two thousand years, and Israel, God's chosen people, for the most part have been blinded to the Gospel. God is turning His face and favor (grace) back to the Jewish people and the time of the gentiles is coming to an end. Of course, God is still with His gentile saints who are faithful to Him, but the time of harvest for the gentiles is coming to an end. Just like God hardened Pharaoh's heart and brought judgment on all of Egypt, I believe Scripture is showing us here that God will be hardening the hearts of those who have hardened their own hearts and refused to repent while there was still time before the judgment of the world. Next, a deeper dive into the Seventh Trumpet.

THE SEVENTH TRUMPET

REVELATION 11:15-17 (NKJV)
¹⁵ Then the seventh angel sounded: And there were loud voices in heaven, saying, "The kingdoms of this world have become the kingdoms of our Lord and of His Christ, and He shall reign forever and ever!"
¹⁶ And the twenty-four elders who sat before God on their thrones fell on their faces and worshiped God,
¹⁷ saying: "We give You thanks, O Lord God Almighty, The One who is and who was and who is to come, Because You have taken Your great power and reigned.

As we have seen before, the Seventh Trumpet is the beginning of the Lord's reign on the earth and the beginning of the end of the reign of the beast.

REVELATION 11:18 (NKJV)
¹⁸ The nations were angry, and Your wrath has come, And the time of the dead, that they should be judged, And that You should reward Your servants the prophets and the saints, And those who fear Your name, small and great, And should destroy those who destroy the earth."

The Seventh Trumpet is the Resurrection and Rapture but look what else it says— *"and Your wrath has come."* If you remember, the Seventh Trumpet is also the Third Woe with the Fifth and Sixth Trumpets being the First and Second Woes. When you think that something has come, you think it is the beginning. So, from this reference it makes you think that God's wrath has just started, but all three of the Woes are severe judgements from God, and for that matter, so are all Seven Trumpets. The judgements of the Seventh Trumpet and Third Woe start in *Revelation 15:1.*

REVELATION 15:1 (NKJV)
¹ Then I saw another sign in heaven, great and marvelous: seven angels having the seven last plagues, for in them the wrath of God is complete.

This says the Seventh Trumpet and Third Woe Judgements are the last plagues and complete the wrath of God. Notice there are seven plagues that come after the sounding of the Seventh Trumpet, which means the Seventh Trumpet has seven plagues for every one of the previous Trumpet Judgements, but at the sounding of the Seventh Trumpet, it says God's wrath has come. The revealing of the seven last plagues that are the Judgements of the Seventh Trumpet, it says they are the last plagues and the completion of God's wrath. How can something be the last and completion and the beginning all at the same time? For that to be the case, there must be two beginnings. Are there two beginnings to the wrath of God in the book of *Revelation* relating to the Trumpet Judgements? Comparing the Judgements of the Seventh Trumpet to first Sixth Trumpets will help answer this question.

REVELATION 16:1-2 (NKJV)
¹ Then I heard a loud voice from the temple saying to the seven angels, "Go and pour out the bowls of the wrath of God on the earth."
² So the first went and poured out his bowl upon the earth, and a foul and loathsome sore came upon the men who had the mark of the beast and those who worshiped his image.

Notice this first bowl is poured out only on those who have the mark of the beast and who worshiped his image, and they are tormented by foul and loathsome sores. This plague has some similarities to the Fifth Trumpet in that only the people who do not belong to Christ are tormented, but in this case, those who have the mark of the beast instead of those who do not have the seal of God, because the mark of the beast is not implemented until sometime during the Sixth Trumpet. This is after the sounding of the Seventh Trumpet, so those with the seal of God will have just been Raptured.

REVELATION 16:3-4 (NKJV)
³ Then the second angel poured out his bowl on the sea, and it became blood as of a dead man; and every living creature in the sea died.
⁴ Then the third angel poured out his bowl on the rivers and springs of water, and they became blood.?"

Here we see again, like the Second and Third Trumpets, God is striking the waters, both sea and fresh waters. Just like those plagues, everything in the waters die and leave no drinking water, and in this case, this is a full global judgment, and all waters are now blood and unusable. The Second and Third Trumpets were semi-global, only striking a third of the earth. There are seven of these last plagues called the bowls of the wrath of God, making the Seventh Trumpet plagues not only full global plagues, but up to twenty-one times worse than any of the first Six Trumpets. We can clearly see that all Seven of the Trumpet Judgements are similar and terrible, but the Last Trumpet is many, many times more severe. If it is God's wrath according to Scripture to destroy a nation like Egypt, and cities like Sodom and Gomorrah, how much more is it God's wrath if the judgements affect a third of the world? The Seven Trumpets are revealed after the Seventh Seal is released and the scroll can be opened. The Seven Trumpets are the Judgements of God contained inside the scroll. The last Three Trumpet Judgements, which includes the Seventh Trumpet and its seven last plagues, are the three woes. Any of the Trumpet Judgements are worse than any judgement of God since Noah's flood, and worse than the ten plagues of Egypt, all of which are the wrath of God, which can only mean one thing; all Seven of the Trumpet Judgements are the wrath of God, and the two beginnings are—the First Trumpet, because it is the beginning of the Trumpet Judgements, and the Seventh Trumpet, because Scripture declares God's wrath has come at the Seventh Trumpet. Why does Scripture declare God's wrath has come at the Seventh Trumpet when it began at the First Trumpet? I believe this is why; the first Six Trumpets are God's wrath in part. Put another way, God's wrath was restrained, releasing only one semi-global plague at a time. The Seventh Trumpet has seven full global plagues many times greater than the first Six Trumpet Judgements combined, bringing the full measure and completion of God's wrath. Simply put; at the First Trumpet, God's wrath comes in part, and at the Seventh Trumpet, God's wrath comes in full and is completed.

The Trumpet Judgments are the wrath of God. This means the wrath of God and the Tribulation of the saints run together, up to the sounding of the Seventh Trumpet. The seven last plagues come after the sounding of Seventh Trumpet. All Scripture references to the Rapture and Resurrection reveal they occur at the sounding of the Seventh Trumpet, indicating the saints will be with Christ when the

final wrath of the Seventh Trumpet and Third Woe is poured out in the seven bowl judgments. Still, the first Six Trumpets are still the wrath of God on a semi-global scale and happen at the same time as the Tribulation of the saints, which means the wrath of God against sinners and the wrath of Satan against the saints occur together. The answer to this part of the question—*When is the Rapture?* It is after the first Six Trumpets of God's wrath and before His final wrath of the Seventh Trumpet.

Adding the answers from part two to the answers from part one:

1. The Rapture is at the Coming of the Lord for all of His people, both those who have died and those still alive.
2. The Rapture is at the Last Trumpet of God, which is the Seventh and Last Trumpet of God in the book of Revelation, and the very Last Trumpet of God in the Bible, making it the true Last Trumpet of God.
3. The Rapture immediately follows the Resurrection of the saints.
4. The Rapture is after the Tribulation, which includes the great persecution of the saints by the beast, who is the antichrist.
5. The Rapture is after the first Six Trumpets of God's wrath.

Doesn't Scripture say that we are not appointed unto wrath? Yes, it does, let's see what Scripture has to say about this and what it means to not be appointed unto wrath.

I THESSALONIANS 5:9 (NKJV)
⁹ For God did not appoint us to wrath, but to obtain salvation through our Lord Jesus Christ,

What does it mean to not be appointed to wrath? This verse says it is to obtain salvation through Jesus Christ. So, what are we being saved from? Scripture says it is appointed to man once to die and then the judgment. Since all men are appointed to physical death, we know this salvation does not mean the saving of our physical bodies. Then the judgment, *Revelation 20* says the final judgment for sinners, the unsaved, is the second death and the lake of fire. So, our salvation and the wrath we are not appointed to is from the second death and the lake of fire. With that, we also know God can and does protect His people

from His wrath, often right in the mist of the judgment as He did with the Israelites in Egypt, Noah and his family in the flood, which was a global judgement, Lot and his family escaping the fire and brimstone that fell on Sodom and Gomorrah, Shadrach, Meshach, and Abed-Nego protected right in the middle of a fiery furnace heated to seven times hotter than normal, and many other times God has protected His people from His wrath.

Studying through the Trumpet Judgments by comparing their similarities to past judgements where God did protect His people, and the Fifth Trumpet of the demonic locusts, Scripture is clear that this judgment is not against His true saints but only against the people who do not have the seal God.

REVELATION 9:3-4 (NKJV)
3 Then out of the smoke locusts came upon the earth. And to them was given power, as the scorpions of the earth have power.
4 They were commanded not to harm the grass of the earth, or any green thing, or any tree, but only those men who do not have the seal of God on their foreheads.

With Scripture as our guide, not being appointed to wrath ultimately means escaping the second death—the lake fire, but it also means God can and does protect the people that are truly His. There is not a single case in Scripture where God removes or has to remove His people from the earth itself to protect them, because He has the power to protect them right in middle of the fire or plague or any other type of Judgment. *Psalm 91* is a perfect picture of this. I believe we need to understand how and why the saints throughout Scripture have escaped God's wrath. It can help us be prepared when God's wrath does come, and we can escape the judgements being poured out on the ungodly. We will start by looking at the many warnings about these times that will help us know what we need to do to escape the wrath to come and endure the time of Tribulation. That brings us to the next question, which I wanted to wait until this point to answer because we have now answered all the questions leading up to the Rapture. Why is it important to know the *Truth about the Rapture?* After having learned so much about the Rapture, we should be coming to an understanding of this, but I believe it is a good idea to closely examine the many warnings in Scripture and to look at them together so we can see the magnitude of these warnings. With that, let's begin to answer this next question.

QUESTION 9

WHY IS THE TRUTH ABOUT THE RAPTURE IMPORTANT?

First, let's look at the similar warnings we are given by Jesus and Paul about the timing of the Rapture and the times leading up to the Rapture. We will start with Paul's warning in *2 Thessalonians 2*.

1 THESSALONIANS 2:1-3 (NKJV)
1 Now, brethren, concerning the coming of our Lord Jesus Christ and our gathering together to Him, we ask you,
2 not to be soon shaken in mind or troubled, either by spirit or by word or by letter, as if from us, as though the day of Christ had come.
3 Let no one deceive you by any means; for that Day will not come unless the falling away comes first, and the man of sin is revealed, the son of perdition,

We have looked at this verse before and we know that Paul is talking about the Rapture here. He says not to be shaken or troubled as if the day of Christ had come, indicating that it has not come. The warning Paul gives here, *"let no one deceive you."* Why did he say that? For one, they had already been deceived into thinking the Rapture had already happened. I believe Paul was also emphasizing that it was important to not be deceived about the timing of the Rapture, and he goes on to tell them of the things that must happen first before the Rapture can happen. Paul understood the seriousness of the times leading up to Rapture and he wanted them to understand how it is important not to be deceived. Jesus also gave warnings not to be deceived in His teachings about the end of the age and His coming, which includes the Rapture.

WARNINGS FROM JESUS

FIRST WARNING

MATTHEW 24:3-4 (NKJV)
3 Now as He sat on the Mount of Olives, the disciples came to Him privately, saying, "Tell us, when will these things be? And what will be the sign of Your coming, and of the end of the age?"
4 And Jesus answered and said to them: "Take heed that no one deceives you."

The disciples are specifically asking the Lord about the sign of His coming and about the end of the age. The very first warning Jesus gives them is to be careful not to be deceived. Note, of all the times in the New Testament where it says not to be deceived, or that people will be deceived, most of those Scriptures are about the coming of the Lord, the Rapture, and the events leading up to them. I believe there is a very important reason why there are so many warnings about not being deceived, or that many will be deceived, and that is Jesus and Paul both knew that Satan was going to cause a great deception about these in order to cause many to not take heed to the many warnings about these times.

Question—What is the opposite of being deceived? Knowing the truth, of course. Therefore, since the Lord and the Apostle Paul have made an emphasis on not being deceived about the coming of the Lord and the Rapture, we should give special attention on knowing the truth about them. Next, we will look at the many warnings in Scripture about these events that will help us understanding why it is so important to know *the Whole Truth about the Rapture.* Jesus, while teaching His disciples about these events, gives them many warnings.

SECOND WARNING

MATTHEW 24:5 (NKJV)
5 For many will come in My name, saying, 'I am the Christ,' and will deceive many.

The first thing the Lord warned His disciples not to be deceived about was His coming. He said many would come in His name and claim to be Christ. Later in this chapter the Lord says that when He comes back, He will be coming from heaven and will light up the sky where everyone will see Him.

THIRD WARNING

MATTHEW 24:6-8 (NKJV)
6 And you will hear of wars and rumors of wars. See that you are not troubled; for all these things must come to pass, but the end is not yet.
7 For nation will rise against nation, and kingdom against kingdom. And there will be famines, pestilences, and earthquakes in various places.
8 All these are the beginning of sorrows.

In this warning, the Lord says when you hear of wars and rumors of wars caused by an increase in nations going to war with other nations, famines and pestilences will also increase, as well as earthquakes in different places all over the world. Jesus says that these are the beginning of sorrows, but not to be worried because all these things must happen before the end. Why would the Lord tell us not to worry when all these terrible things will happen before the end? This is what I believe; First, worry is fear and the opposite of faith, and it prevents us from trusting the Lord to get us through whatever comes. Second, wars, famines, pestilence, and earthquakes are judgments (wrath) of God against the wicked. The saints are holy, these judgments are not against them, and God can and will, for many, protect them and get them through these times if they will trust and obey Him and not give in to fear and sin. The word of the Lord by Zephaniah the Prophet on how to prepare to escape the wrath of God—

ZEPHANIAH 2:2-3 (NKJV)
² Before the decree is issued, Or the day passes like chaff, Before the Lord's fierce anger comes upon you, Before the day of the Lord's anger comes upon you!
³ Seek the Lord, all you meek of the earth, Who have upheld His justice. Seek righteousness, seek humility. It may be that you will be hidden In the day of the Lord's anger.

We cannot wait until God's wrath comes to seek the Lord, or righteousness and humility. *Isaiah 55:6-7* says to seek the Lord while He may be found. We need to seek the Lord while there is still time. If we truly heed these warnings from the Lord with all our hearts, we can expect what is written in *Psalm 91*.

PSALM 91:1-7 (NKJV)
¹ He who dwells in the secret place of the Most High Shall abide under the shadow of the Almighty.
² I will say of the Lord, "He is my refuge and my fortress; My God, in Him I will trust."
³ Surely He shall deliver you from the snare of the fowler And from the perilous pestilence.
⁴ He shall cover you with His feathers, And under His wings you shall take refuge; His truth shall be your shield and buckler.
⁵ You shall not be afraid of the terror by night, Nor of the arrow that flies by day,
⁶ Nor of the pestilence that walks in darkness, Nor of the destruction that lays waste at noonday.
⁷ A thousand may fall at your side, And ten thousand at your right hand; But it shall not come near you.

FOURTH WARNING

MATTHEW 24:9-11 (NKJV)
9 "Then they will deliver you up to tribulation and kill you, and you will be hated by all nations for My name's sake.
10 And then many will be offended, will betray one another, and will hate one another.
11 Then many false prophets will rise up and deceive many.

The beginning of sorrows, which are the birth pains, will eventually give birth to the Tribulation. When the Lord was teaching His disciples about the Tribulation, He specifically said it would happen to His disciples who are alive at the time, and therefore, the Tribulation is actually the Tribulation of the saints. The birth pains were the beginning of God's judgements against the wicked, but the Tribulation is the devil and the wicked people persecuting the saints and is something most saints alive at the time will have to endure. Jesus warns that they will kill them, and they will be hated by all the nations for His name's sake because we belong to Christ. The reason they will hate us is because the saints will be living holy lives, not participating in the wicked ways of the world. Because the judgements of God are not against His people who walk in holiness but against the wicked people of the world, there will be a distinction between how these judgements affect the people of the world and God's righteous ones. The world, like Egypt, is going to see that difference and will hate God's people. The Lord also warned that many in the company of the saints who fall away will be offended, hate them, and betray the saints. These will be the most terrible times for the saints of God. The Lord has warned us that these things will happen. He will not forsake His people, but He will allow us to suffer this for His glory and our reward at the Resurrection and Rapture and for all eternity.

In the next two verses, Jesus gives the reason why many fall away, and that reason is the key in how not to fall away. This is a very important key, so we are going to dive deep into it so we can learn how to prepare ourselves and not be among those who fall away.

FIFTH WARNING

MATTHEW 24:12-13 (NKJV)

¹² And because lawlessness will abound, the love of many will grow cold.
¹³ But he who endures to the end shall be saved.

Jesus says, because lawlessness (wickedness) will abound, meaning it will greatly increase everywhere, the love of many will grow cold, but the one who endures to the end will be saved. Jesus also taught that God's law is summed up in two commands; Love God with all your heart and love your neighbor as yourself. So, love is the fulfillment of God's law, which makes sense. As lawlessness increases, love is going to decrease. He is certainly talking about the whole world here, but He is directing this warning to His followers. He makes it clear, without love we will not be able to endure to the end and be saved. Whether that end is death or the Rapture, the one who does not make it to the end without falling into the wickedness of the world will not be saved. This then is the question—How do we keep the lawlessness, which is inevitable, from causing our love to growing cold? Lawlessness is sin and the opposite of love, so the more we get sin out of our lives the stronger our love will grow, and loving others as Jesus commanded will cause our love to grow stronger. Let's start with how we get sin out of our life. I believe Jesus provided good answers to this question in the Gospels.

MATTHEW 10:28 (NKJV)

²⁸ And do not fear those who kill the body but cannot kill the soul. But rather fear Him who is able to destroy both soul and body in hell.

The Lord is teaching us to fear God and not fear man or the devil who can only kill the body, because only God has the power and authority to cast us into hell. *Proverbs 9:10* says, *"The fear of the Lord is the beginning of wisdom."* The highest wisdom is to love God with all your heart, but you cannot get to the end of something without starting at the beginning. A foundation is the beginning of a house, and the quality and strength of that foundation will determine if the house can stand through storms or not. Jesus taught this in *Matthew 7:24-27*. Since

the fear of the Lord is the beginning of wisdom, it is the foundation of our wisdom, and to reach the highest wisdom, to love God with all our hearts, we need to build a strong foundation of the fear of the Lord. How do we make the fear of God greater than the fear of man or the devil? By truly believing what Jesus said, that God is the only one who has the power to destroy both our body and soul in hell for all eternity. Our lives in this world are short and the suffering temporary, the punishment for sin is far worse than any suffering in this world and it will last forever. The fear of God is a very good thing because it motivates us to repent and overcome sin, giving us the hope of escaping the punishment our sin deserves, and instead, have eternal life in heaven. *Proverbs 29:25* says, *"The fear of man brings a snare,"* the fear of man will snare and trap you in sin and death. In the next passage, the Lord continues to teach us how serious we should take fearing God and getting sin out of our lives.

MATTHEW 18:8-9 (NKJV)

8 "If your hand or foot causes you to sin, cut it off and cast it from you. It is better for you to enter into life lame or maimed, rather than having two hands or two feet, to be cast into the everlasting fire.

9 And if your eye causes you to sin, pluck it out and cast it from you. It is better for you to enter into life with one eye, rather than having two eyes, to be cast into hell fire.

The Bible says our body is the temple of the Holy Spirit and we are not to destroy it, *1 Corinthians 3:17, 6:19.* The Lord is not telling us to destroy our bodies, but is using that as an extreme example of how serious we should take getting sin out of our lives, that we would be better off if our bodies were destroyed in an effort to overcome sin than being cast into hell fire where we will be destroyed forever. Since the Lord is giving us the ultimate consequences for not overcoming, then overcoming sin should be our ultimate goal. There are two Scriptures in the book of *Revelation* that emphasizes how important it is to overcome sin.

REVELATION 2:11 (NKJV)

11 "He who has an ear, let him hear what the Spirit says to the Churches. He who overcomes shall not be hurt by the second death."

REVELATION 3:5 (NKJV)

5 He who overcomes shall be clothed in white garments, and I will not blot out his name from the Book of Life; but I will confess his name before My Father and before His angels.

Now, in these two verses, Jesus says he who overcomes will not be hurt by the second death, which is the lake of fire, and He will not blot out their name from the book of life. The person whose name is blotted out of the book of life on Judgment Day is cast into the lake of fire, *Revelation 20:15*. That is twice where Jesus says that the overcomer will be safe from the eternal destruction of the lake of fire. On the other side of this, the one who does not overcome is not safe from eternal destruction and is in danger of hellfire.

Scripture is very clear; we need to fear God and make every effort to overcome sin. To become a true Christian, a person must repent of their sins, but many Christians still struggle with sin after their conversion, many to the point that they have to repent of sin regularly when they stumble or fall and continue to work with the Lord to overcome them. I believe this pleases the Lord, as long as we continue to prayerfully work with Him to overcome our sins, but, if we quit and accept our sin and continue in it with no real effort to overcome, I believe this displeases the Lord and we will begin to backslide and could eventually fall away. I also believe this, if you do not quit and continue to repent and work with the Lord, you will overcome. From these Scriptures, it is very clear the Lord is teaching us that we not only need to make an effort to overcome sin but make an extreme effort to overcome sin. What else does Scripture teach that we can apply to help prevent our love from growing cold?

1 JOHN 2:15-17 (NKJV)

15 Do not love the world or the things in the world. If anyone loves the world, the love of the Father is not in him. 16 For all that is in the world—the lust of the flesh, the lust of the eyes, and the pride of life—is not of the Father but is of the world. 17 And the world is passing away, and the lust of it; but he who does the will of God abides forever.

This word is clear; if we love the world, God's love is not in us. Notice how this passage describes the love of the world as being lust. Lust is the opposite of the love of God, which is giving and unselfish and it places the needs of others above selfish interests. Lust, on the other hand, because of its self-serving passion, causes us to believe it is love, but it is not! True love is not selfish or self-seeking! *Verse 16* describes the three major categories of the love (lusts) of the world, and they are the lust of the flesh, the lust of the eyes, and the pride of life. The lusts of the flesh are sexual lust, gluttony, drunkenness, drug addiction, and self-indulgence of the flesh that goes against the word of God. The lusts of the eyes can also be sexual lust, it is covetousness, greed and selfish desires for anything we want, an over admiration, a type of worship for beautiful things both man-made and natural, including the stars, the moon, etc. The pride of life is being prideful of the things we possess, our accomplishments, and anything else we are proud of instead of being grateful to God for them. These three sum up the love of the world, and as it says, if this is the love that your heart and life are full of, then you do not have the love of God, or you have very little of it. Without the love of God, there is no way your heart is not going to grow cold and hard and you are not going to be able to endure to the end so you can be saved, and you will easily fall into the traps and snares of the evil one. Very few people do not struggle with these, overcoming sin is a struggle, but there would be no real victory without a real a battle.

We are warned, as the end is approaching, the love of many is going to grow cold. Now is the time to wrestle with these demons and selfish desires and purify our hearts so we will be overcomers. Jesus also has something to say about loving the world and I believe it is very important we look at what He has to say.

SIXTH WARNING

MATTHEW 6:24 (NKJV)

²⁴ "No one can serve two masters; for either he will hate the one and love the other, or else he will be loyal to the one and despise the other. You cannot serve God and mammon."

"Mammon" is the wealth of world, and Jesus says you cannot serve God and worldly wealth. He goes on to say that you will hate one and love the other, associating what you serve to what you love. This confirms what we just learn in the preceding passages of Scripture, if you love the world, you do not have the love of God in your heart, and instead of God's love, you hate God. Hate is a strong word, but what Jesus is saying is that you cannot love both. You will either love one or the other, and the one you do not love you actually hate. I believe Jesus taught this because He knows how deceptive the heart is. When people are not under a lot of pressure to choose between God and worldly wealth, they will try and serve both, and since they are not being pressured to choose, they may not realize what they truly love and are loyal to, or what they truly do not love and are not loyal to. When the pressure of choice comes, their true love and loyalty will be exposed and they will turn against the other, even revealing their hatred for the other. Remember, Jesus said love can grow cold, meaning we can start out loving one more than the other, but as we give ourselves more and more to one, our devotion can shift to the other.

The Bible says the heart is deceptive and wicked, *Jeremiah 17:9*. We cannot trust our hearts, we need to trust the Lord and make sure He is our true love and devotion with prayer and diligence, otherwise we may wind up with our devotion being to the world and its wealth. Jesus says it plainly, you cannot serve God and worldly wealth, but most of us have to work for a living, so how do we manage that? We put Him and His kingdom first, make Him the priority in our lives and submit all our worldly wealth to His Will and do what He commands us to do with it. We have looked at what causes our love to grow cold and how to prevent it, now we will look at what can help our love grow stronger.

JOHN 3:16-17 (NKJV)

[16] For God so loved the world that He gave His only begotten Son, that whoever believes in Him should not perish but have everlasting life.
[17] For God did not send His Son into the world to condemn the world, but that the world through Him might be saved.

The greatest love ever shown is God giving His only begotten Son, and Jesus, the Son of God, laying down His life for us. Jesus tells us how we can live the greatest love possible for a human being.

JOHN 15:13 (NKJV)

[13] Greater love has no one than this, than to lay down one's life for his friends.

Just as the Son of God's greatest act of love was to lay down His life, the Lord says our love is greatest when we lay down our lives for others. Laying down one's life is an extreme act and does not always mean to die, but it does mean to sacrifice our life for God and others. The attributes of love are found in *1 Corinthians 13*.

1 CORINTHIANS 13:4-7 (NKJV)

[4] Love is patient, love is kind. It does not envy, it does not boast, it is not proud.
[5] It does not dishonor others, it is not self-seeking, it is not easily angered, it keeps no record of wrongs.
[6] Love does not delight in evil but rejoices with the truth.
[7] It always protects, always trusts, always hopes, always perseveres.

If we examine ourselves in light of the truths we have learned about God's love, it can help us determine where our hearts really are so we can make the necessary changes in our lives while we still have the time and grace to do so. Because of the very serious fact that many will fall away, we have thoroughly examined this key that the Lord gave us, to understand why many will fall away and what we must do to prepare ourselves so that we do not fall away but endure to the end.

SEVENTH WARNING

MATTHEW 24:15-18,21-22 (NKJV)

15 "Therefore when you see the 'abomination of desolation,' spoken of by Daniel the prophet, standing in the holy place" (whoever reads, let him understand),

16 "then let those who are in Judea flee to the mountains.

17 Let him who is on the housetop not go down to take anything out of his house.

18 And let him who is in the field not go back to get his clothes.

21 For then there will be great tribulation, such as has not been since the beginning of the world until this time, no, nor ever shall be.

22 And unless those days were shortened, no flesh would be saved; but for the elect's sake those days will be shortened.

Sometime during the beast's three-and-a-half-year global rein and his war with the saints, he will setup the image of the beast, which is the abomination of desolation, and demand everyone in the world worship the image of the beast, and he is going to kill everyone who does not worship the image of the beast.

REVELATION 13:15 (NKJV)

15 He was granted power to give breath to the image of the beast, that the image of the beast should both speak and cause as many as would not worship the image of the beast to be killed.

Since the beast will have authority over all the nations, he will be able to kill everyone in every nation very quickly. Jesus says this will be the Greatest Tribulation ever and warns us not to go home for any reason, but instead, flee to the mountains. He says if He does not shorten those days, no flesh will be saved. He says He is going to shorten those days for the sake of the elect. In Jesus' teaching about the Tribulation and His return, the time of the abomination of desolation is one of the very last events, with that time being so terrible that the Lord has to shorten it so that all flesh is not destroyed. Along with the fact that the global rein of the beast is only forty-two months, it is very

likely that this event is not only toward the end of the Great Tribulation but it will not last very long. We will learn more about the timing of when the abomination of desolation is setup in the next chapter.

EIGHTH WARNING

MATTHEW 24:23-27 (NKJV)

23 "Then if anyone says to you, 'Look, here is the Christ!' or 'There!' do not believe it.

24 For false christs and false prophets will rise and show great signs and wonders to deceive, if possible, even the elect.

25 See, I have told you beforehand.

26 "Therefore if they say to you, 'Look, He is in the desert!' do not go out; or 'Look, He is in the inner rooms!' do not believe it.

27 For as the lightning comes from the east and flashes to the west, so also will the coming of the Son of Man be.

Jesus says, then if anyone says Christ is here or there, do not believe it. The first word in this warning is "then," which also means at that time, and that time is the time Jesus was just teaching about, which was the Great Tribulation and the setting up of the abomination of desolation (the image of the beast). Which means the time He was teaching about is the forty-two-month global rein of the beast, where together with the false prophet he causes the Tribulation of the saints. Jesus continues and says, at that time false christs and false prophets will perform great signs and wonders to deceive the world, and if possible, even the saints. The Lord was warning us about the beast and the false prophet and told us not to believe it if someone says that Christ is here or there, or in the desert or the inner rooms. When Christ comes, He is going to light up the sky and will be coming from heaven. The Lord said he has told us ahead of time. The book of *Revelation* reveals more details about the false christ and the false prophet.

REVELATION 13:11-15 (NKJV)

11 Then I saw another beast coming up out of the earth, and he had two horns like a lamb and spoke like a dragon.

¹² And he exercises all the authority of the first beast in his presence, and causes the earth and those who dwell in it to worship the first beast, whose deadly wound was healed.
¹³ He performs great signs, so that he even makes fire come down from heaven on the earth in the sight of men.
¹⁴ And he deceives those who dwell on the earth by those signs which he was granted to do in the sight of the beast, telling those who dwell on the earth to make an image to the beast who was wounded by the sword and lived.
¹⁵ He was granted power to give breath to the image of the beast, that the image of the beast should both speak and cause as many as would not worship the image of the beast to be killed.

This passage reveals that the second beast, who is the false prophet, does exactly what Jesus said he would do, he performed great signs and wonders to deceive the whole world into worshiping the beast, who is the false christ. Then he tells all the people of the world to make an image of the beast, the abomination of desolation, and with satanic power causes the image to both breathe and speak. As we just recently learned, what happens when the abomination of desolation is setup? He kills everyone on the earth who will not worship the abomination of desolation, causing the greatest persecution ever for the saints. The true saints of God will not worship the beast or his image. *Revelation 19:20* reveals that the second beast is the false prophet.

NINTH WARNING

MATTHEW 24:29-31 (NKJV)
²⁹ "Immediately after the Tribulation of those days the sun will be darkened, and the moon will not give its light; the stars will fall from heaven, and the powers of the heavens will be shaken.
³⁰ Then the sign of the Son of Man will appear in heaven, and then all the tribes of the earth will mourn, and they will see the Son of Man coming on the clouds of heaven with power and great glory.

³¹ And He will send His angels with a great sound of a trumpet, and they will gather together His elect from the four winds, from one end of heaven to the other.

MARK 13:24-27 (NKJV)

²⁴ "But in those days, after that tribulation, the sun will be darkened, and the moon will not give its light;
²⁵ the stars of heaven will fall, and the powers in the heavens will be shaken.
²⁶ Then they will see the Son of Man coming in the clouds with great power and glory.
²⁷ And then He will send His angels, and gather together His elect from the four winds, from the farthest part of earth to the farthest part of heaven.

After the saints have endured the Great Tribulation caused by the beast and his followers, the very last events will take place. The sun will be darkened, and the moon will not give its light. From the Sixth Seal and other verses we know the moon will actually be blood red and will be visible, but not bright enough to shine its light on the earth. There will falling stars and the heavens will be shaken. Since these are the very last events, the saints still alive will know the Lord is getting ready to light up the sky and everyone is going to see Him when He comes. Then, He is going to, with the help of His angels, resurrect all the saints who have died and bring them to Him, and they will receive their new glorified bodies, and then with the help of His angels, He is going to Rapture all the saints still alive, and they will be transformed into their new glorified bodies and will meet Him in the sky. The warning that we should take from this is something we have already learned, but we need to take it as a warning as well. The Rapture is not until after the Tribulation, which means we need to prepare our minds, hearts, and lives to endure the Tribulation until the end.

TENTH WARNING

MATTHEW 24:32-35 (NKJV)

[32] "Now learn this parable from the fig tree: When its branch has already become tender and puts forth leaves, you know that summer is near.
[33] So you also, when you see all these things, know that it is near—at the doors!
[34] Assuredly, I say to you, this generation will by no means pass away till all these things take place.
[35] heaven and earth will pass away, but My words will by no means pass away.

The Lord says, when you see all these things, including the last events of the sun being darkened and the moon not giving its light, and the power of the heavens shaken, His coming is very near, right at the door, so if you are a saint still alive on the earth, you can begin to rejoice because He will soon light up the sky and you are going to see Him coming.

Warning: He's not coming back until all these events take place. Remember, these are His words, heaven and earth will pass away but His words will not fail. They will come to pass, no matter what.

A list of all the events Jesus says will happen before His coming.

1. Continuous increase in wars, famines, pestilences, and earthquakes. But the end is not yet, this is the beginning of the birth pains.
2. Saints are killed and hated by all the nations.
3. In the company of the saints, people will be offended, betray and hate each other.
4. False christs and false prophets will arise, with the beast and the false prophet as the final false christ and false prophet.
5. The mark of the beast and the inability to buy or sell without the mark.
6. The abomination of desolation (the image of the beast).
7. The sun is darkened, and the moon does not give its light, and the power of the heavens are shaken.

As we see a continuous increase in wars, famines, pestilences, and earthquakes, we know we are getting closer to the Tribulation of the saints where the saints are killed and hated by all the nations. People will be offended, betray and hate each other, including believers that have fallen away. You can be certain that those who fall away and persecute the true believers will experience God's wrath. The steadfast believers may be protected from God's wrath, but many will experience the wrath of Satan through the beast and his followers. Remember, it was the religious people of Christ's time that persecuted Him and had Him killed!

This exactly what Jesus warned us would happen to those who did not watch and were not ready, they would start abusing their fellow servants. The beast-antichrist and his false prophet will come to global power for the last three-and-a-half years and he will ultimately setup the abomination of desolation, which is the image of the beast, and order all those who won't worship this satanic statue to be killed.

ELEVENTH WARNING

MATTHEW 24:36-39 (NKJV)
36 "But of that day and hour no one knows, not even the angels of heaven, but My Father only.
37 But as the days of Noah were, so also will the coming of the Son of Man be.
38 For as in the days before the flood, they were eating and drinking, marrying and giving in marriage, until the day that Noah entered the ark,
39 and did not know until the flood came and took them all away, so also will the coming of the Son of Man be.

The Lord says that no one knows the day or hour of His coming, but he did teach us in previous passages all the events, including the final events of what will take place right before He comes. Even though we do not know the exact day or hour, as these events unfold and come closer to completion, we will know it is near because the Lord told us we would know in *Matthew 24:33* when it is near. Jesus said, before He comes, the days will be like the days of Noah, the days of Noah are found in *Genesis 6-8*. It teaches that mankind had become completely wicked, and God destroyed them from the face of the earth with a great flood except for Noah and his family of eight. Scripture tells us why Noah escaped the flood and what his attitude and actions were before the coming of the flood.

GENESIS 6:9 (NKJV)
9 Noah was a just man, perfect in his generations. Noah walked with God.

HEBREWS 11:7 (NKJV)
7 By faith Noah, being divinely warned of things not yet seen, moved with godly fear, prepared an ark for the saving of his household, by which he condemned the world and became heir of the righteousness which is according to faith.

Scripture says Noah was a just and perfect man who walked with God, though no man is truly perfect except Jesus Christ, I believe the word perfect was used here to describe Noah as a truly godly and righteous man who walked with God. Noah's attitude and actions were that he believed in the divine warning of a global judgement that has never been seen before, which would not come for more than a hundred years, and he moved with godly fear and obeyed what he was instructed to do. In that obedience, he built the ark and escaped the wrath to come. In this we can see the importance of having a real faith in divine warnings, and all of Scripture is divine, which means all the warnings in Scripture are divine warnings. It is important to fear God and obey what He instructs us to do so we can be prepared to escape His wrath. Next is the other judgement of God that Jesus compared with the time of His coming, warning us of what that time would be like.

LUKE 17:28-30,32 (NKJV)
28 Likewise as it was also in the days of Lot: They ate, they drank, they bought, they sold, they planted, they built;
29 but on the day that Lot went out of Sodom it rained fire and brimstone from heaven and destroyed them all.
30 Even so will it be in the day when the Son of Man is revealed.
32 **Remember Lot's wife.**

This passage describes the day when Lot, Abraham's nephew, went out of the city of Sodom where God rained fire and brimstone down from heaven and destroyed them and all the surrounding cities. At the end of this passage, it very specifically warns us to remember Lot's wife. For that reason, let's read the actual event as it unfolded in Scripture.

GENESIS 19:17,26 (NKJV)

[17] So it came to pass, when they had brought them outside, that he said, "Escape for your life! Do not look behind you nor stay anywhere in the plain. Escape to the mountains, lest you be destroyed."
[26] But his wife looked back behind him, and she became a pillar of salt.

After Lot and his family were brought to the outside of the city, the two angels specifically told them not look behind them, but as it says, Lot's wife looked back, and she became a pillar of salt. So, why did Jesus compare the days of His coming to the destruction of Sodom and Gomorrah? The destruction of Sodom and Gomorrah, just like the flood in Noah's time, were the wrath of God. Jesus wants us to understand that the days of His coming will be a time of the wrath of God. He gave a very specific warning about what happened to Lot's wife, which He was referring to her disobedience, and her demise. Scripture tells us that Lot was a righteous man and God often spares the righteous from His wrath. As it was in this case, Lot and his family escaped God's wrath, but his wife is destroyed for one act of disobedience. What I believe Jesus is teaching us here is that He spares the righteous from His wrath, but extreme obedience is required leading up to it, as with the case of Noah moving in the fear of God and obeying long before the wrath came. During the times of God's wrath, as with the case of Lot and his family, the disobedient will not escape His wrath. What does all this mean for the last day saints during these times? Taking from what we learned from Noah and Lot, we need to believe the warnings given by God, and in the holy fear of God obey the instructions given in these warnings, understanding that disobedience is not an option. With that, be prepared to escape the wrath to come.

Notice these warnings of global judgement. The instructions and required obedience, in the case of Noah, was given long before the flood. In the case of Lot and his family, it was right at the time of the judgement. In either case, disobedience is not an option in regard to times of God's wrath. It is true, we are living in the time of grace, which is a time of repentance and forgiveness, but when God's wrath comes, the time of grace will be over. We need to repent and obey God's commands and heed all the warnings in Scripture concerning these times while we have the grace and not wait until it is too late to escape the wrath to come. This sounds so serious, and it is serious! I believe Jesus was very serious in His warnings about these times. If Lot's wife perished because she disobeyed the two angels, how much more danger are we going to be in if we do not heed the warnings of the Son of God, who is the Word of God? Before we look at the other warnings given in Scripture about these times that we should obey, we will look at some other Scriptures that makes clear how serious the time of God's wrath is, even for His own people.

EZEKIEL 14:19-20 (NKJV)

19 "Or if I send a pestilence into that land and pour out My fury on it in blood, and cut off from it man and beast,
20 even though Noah, Daniel, and Job were in it, as I live," says the Lord God, "they would deliver neither son nor daughter; they would deliver only themselves by their righteousness."

Ezekiel 14:12-20 describes how serious it is when God brings His judgement against a land. The passage says it twice that Noah, Daniel, and Job, who are three of the most righteous men in all of Scripture, cannot keep their own sons or daughters from destruction. In a time of God's wrath, they can only save themselves by their righteousness. This passage makes one thing very clear; God's wrath is a time to take very seriously since He is only going to spare the truly righteous, and even the most godly will not be able to keep their own unrighteous children from destruction. The good news is, God always warns us about His coming wrath, and with those warnings come opportunities to repent and obey, and often very specific instructions to obey in order to escape the wrath to come.

I PETER 4:17-18 (KJV)
¹⁷ For the time has come for judgment to begin at the house of God; and if it begins with us first, what will be the end of those who do not obey the Gospel of God?
¹⁸ Now "If the righteous one is scarcely saved, Where will the ungodly and the sinner appear?"

This passage says judgement begins with the house God, so God is going to judge His own house in this world first to remove the tares and ungodly, like Lot's wife. With all that we studied, we can see that when God's judgement comes, it is a very serious thing not to be taken lightly. Like Noah, we need to move with the fear of God and obey the warnings and instructions given to us through Scripture and God's holy prophets.

The Lord specifically mentions the actions of the people right before the flood came and destroyed them all, and right before the fire and brimstone poured down and destroyed Sodom and Gomorrah and the surrounding cities. They were eating, drinking, and marrying. One thing we need to understand is the global flood and the burning of Sodom and Gomorrah are the wrath of God, and they are not just God's wrath but God's wrath of total destruction of people that are completely wicked. At the Seventh Trumpet when the saints still alive are caught up to meet the Lord, almost everyone left on the earth is going to be a follower of the beast and will be very wicked. Like before Noah entered the ark, people will be eating, drinking, and marrying, then sudden and total destruction will come upon them like the flood that destroyed everyone on the earth except Noah and his family, and the fire and brimstone that completely destroyed Sodom and Gomorrah and the surrounding cities. God is going to pour out the judgment of the Seventh Trumpet and Third Woe, which is the Seven Bowls and are the full measure of the wrath of God. A wrath of total destruction like Noah's flood and Sodom and Gomorrah. Even though the first Six Trumpet Judgements will come before the Lord's coming at the Seventh Trumpet, they are not a wrath of the total destruction of the wicked like what is going to come after the Seventh Trumpet. The people of the world, not the Tribulation saints, are going to try as much as possible to live normal lives, such as eating, drinking, and marrying, even during

the Sixth Trumpet when the beast rules for forty-two months. They, with the beast, will wage war against the saints, and then a sudden global scale destruction will come upon them like a thief in the night.

1 THESSALONIANS 5:2-3,9 (NKJV)

² For you yourselves know perfectly that the day of the Lord so comes as a thief in the night.

³ For when they say, "Peace and safety!" then sudden destruction comes upon them, as labor pains upon a pregnant woman. And they shall not escape.

⁹ For God did not appoint us to wrath, but to obtain salvation through our Lord Jesus Christ,

What the Apostle Paul tells the Church in Thessalonica agrees with what Jesus taught His disciples, that the people of the world will go on living life as normal and will be saying *"peace and safety!"* under the rule of the beast. Then suddenly, and total destruction will come upon the kingdom of the beast and his followers after the Lord comes for his saints. Paul also says we are not appointed to wrath, and that is correct, the saints will escape this full global wrath of God when the Lord comes, and they will be able to escape the wrath of God of the first Six Trumpets by being protected like Noah and Lot were if they continue in faith and strict obedience to God. The saints will suffer some during the first Six Trumpets, just like Noah who was stuck on an ark for almost a year, and like Lot who lost his home, all his property, and his wife. But these judgements are intended for the wicked people of the world, and they won't just suffer, many will be destroyed by them until the final judgement comes and destroys them all.

TWELFTH WARNING

MATTHEW 24:42-51 (NKJV)

[42] Watch therefore, for you do not know what hour your Lord is coming.

[43] But know this, that if the master of the house had known what hour the thief would come, he would have watched and not allowed his house to be broken into.

[44] Therefore you also be ready, for the Son of Man is coming at an hour you do not expect.

[45] "Who then is a faithful and wise servant, whom his master made ruler over his household, to give them food in due season?

[46] Blessed is that servant whom his master, when he comes, will find so doing.

[47] Assuredly, I say to you that he will make him ruler over all his goods.

[48] But if that evil servant says in his heart, 'My master is delaying his coming,'

[49] and begins to beat his fellow servants, and to eat and drink with the drunkards,

[50] the master of that servant will come on a day when he is not looking for him and at an hour that he is not aware of,

[51] and will cut him in two and appoint him his portion with the hypocrites. There shall be weeping and gnashing of teeth.

The Lord says to watch, for you do not know the hour of His coming. Which is true, but we do know the events that will lead up to His coming and the very last events right before He comes, so we need to watch all these events to help us understand the times and to keep us alert and ready. The Lord is teaching that being watchful is directly related to being ready, and He says to always be ready for His coming, at all times. Why would being watchful help us stay ready for the Lord's coming, even though there are multiple events that have to take place before the Lord's return? That is the answer. Many of the events before the Lord comes are the wrath of God and the Tribulation of the saints, and these could overtake us quickly if we let are guard down and begin to live life any way we want to. We will begin to fall away, which will lead to abusing others and indulge ourselves in the sins of the world, and ultimately failing the calling God has given us. In the end, that person will fall and receive the wrath and judgement of the hypocrites, which is eternal destruction. I believe this; The Lord is warning us to be watchful and ready at all times so we do not fall away, even if He does not come back in our lifetime, because if a person does fall away and does not repent, the Lord could come to that person at any time and cut their life short and appoint them their portion with the hypocrites. If we obey the Lord's commands and remain watchful and ready and fulfill our calling, we will receive great reward at His coming!

WARNINGS FROM THE BOOK OF REVELATION

REVELATION 13:7-10 (NKJV)
7 It was granted to him to make war with the saints and to overcome them. And authority was given him over every tribe, tongue, and nation.
8 All who dwell on the earth will worship him, whose names have not been written in the Book of Life of the Lamb slain from the foundation of the world.
9 If anyone has an ear, let him hear.
10 He who leads into captivity shall go into captivity; he who kills with the sword must be killed with the sword. Here is the patience and the faith of the saints.

Reviewing *verses 7-8*, the beast is going to make war with the saints and will have authority over all the nations and the whole world is going to worship the beast, those whose names are not written in the book of life. Not many are going to escape this great persecution! Next, *verses 9-10* are a warning to all those who have ears to hear. The warning is this; not to take captives (prisoners) and not to kill with the sword (weapons of war), and those who do take captives and kill during the time of the beast-antichrist's global war against the saints, the Great Tribulation, they will be taken captive if they take captives and killed if they kill. Jesus gave a similar warning to His disciples the night of His crucifixion.

MATTHEW 26:52 (NKJV)
⁵² But Jesus said to him, "Put your sword in its place, for all who take the sword will perish by the sword."

Aside from the warning that those who use the sword will die by the sword, there is something else in common with these two warnings, and Jesus said this to His disciples the night He was taken captive to be killed. This warning to the saints is for the time that they will experience great persecution and be taken captive and killed. The last statement in *Revelation 13:10, "Here is the patience and the faith of the saints,"* this warning is instructing the saints to hold onto their faith and endure the persecution, even as Christ our Lord did. Those who take up the sword are not going to have victory by the sword, they are going to lose their lives and die by the sword. In so, taking up the sword benefits them nothing and they forfeit two greater opportunities; The possibility of being protected from the sword, and the glory and reward they would receive from Christ at the Resurrection for laying down their lives for Him. Since Christ had to command His disciple to put his sword away, I believe many will disobey the Lord in a time when strict obedience to the Lord's commands is very important, causing a third possible loss that disobedience to this command could cause them to fall away, especially if their trust is in the sword instead of putting all their faith in Christ. *Matthew 5:39* is another related verse.

MATTHEW 5:39 (NKJV)
³⁹ But I tell you not to resist an evil person. But whoever slaps you on your right cheek, turn the other to him also.

I believe the Lord is calling us to live nonviolent lives. If we, like the disciple in the garden, have a mind that is quick to take up the sword, it may be difficult to react differently when persecution comes. Preparing our hearts and minds with an attitude of nonviolence will be an important way to prepare for a time of great persecution.

REVELATION 18:4 (NKJV)

4 And I heard another voice from heaven saying, "Come out of her, my people, lest you share in her sins, and lest you receive of her plagues.

In this warning from the Lord, He says to *"Come out of her,"* otherwise you will fall into *her sins* and be punished with the plagues she is going to be punished with. In order to escape falling into her sins and receiving her plagues, we are going to have to do whatever is necessary to come out of *her*. To do that, we need to know who *she* is and what her sins are. *Revelation 17 and 18* provide a lot of information on who *she* is, and we will study these to gain the knowledge that we need to know about her.

REVELATION 17:1-5 (NKJV)

1 Then one of the seven angels who had the seven bowls came and talked with me, saying to me, "Come, I will show you the judgment of the great harlot who sits on many waters,
2 with whom the kings of the earth committed fornication, and the inhabitants of the earth were made drunk with the wine of her fornication."
3 So he carried me away in the Spirit into the wilderness. And I saw a woman sitting on a scarlet beast which was full of names of blasphemy, having seven heads and ten horns.
4 The woman was arrayed in purple and scarlet, and adorned with gold and precious stones and pearls, having in her hand a golden cup full of abominations and the filthiness of her fornication.
5 And on her forehead a name was written: MYSTERY, BABYLON THE GREAT, THE MOTHER OF HARLOTS AND OF THE ABOMINATIONS OF THE EARTH.

She is a great prostitute who sits on many waters, the rulers of the earth commit fornication, which is sexual sin, with her, and the people of the world are intoxicated with the potion of her sexual sin. She sits on the red blasphemous beast with the seven heads and ten horns. The woman is dressed in the finest clothes and jewelry with a golden cup in her hand full of abominations and the filthiness of her sexual sins. Her name is written on her forehead, *"MYSTERY, BABYLON THE GREAT, THE MOTHER OF HARLOTS AND OF THE ABOMINATIONS OF THE EARTH."* The name written on her forehead reveals she is a mystery, and her name is Babylon the Great, and that she is the mother of prostitutes and the abominations of the earth.

A list of what we have learned about *her* so far.

1. She is a Mystery.
2. Her name is Babylon the Great.
3. She is the mother of prostitutes and the abominations of the earth.
4. She is very decadent and dresses in the richest clothing and jewelry.
5. She has a golden cup in her hand full of abominations and the filthiness of her sexual sins.
6. The rulers of the earth commit sexual sins with her.
7. The people of the world are intoxicated with her sexual sins.
8. She sits on many waters.
9. She sits on the beast with the seven heads and ten horns.

One thing becomes very clear from this passage, that Babylon is the mother, the source and cause of most, if not all the sexual sins and abominations on the earth. Who is Babylon?

REVELATION 17:6-8 (NKJV)
[6] I saw the woman, drunk with the blood of the saints and with the blood of the martyrs of Jesus. And when I saw her, I marveled with great amazement.
[7] But the angel said to me, "Why did you marvel? I will tell you the mystery of the woman and of the beast that carries her, which has the seven heads and the ten horns.
[8] The beast that you saw was, and is not, and will ascend out of the bottomless pit and go to perdition. And those who dwell on the earth will marvel, whose names are not written in the Book of Life from the foundation of the world, when they see the beast that was, and is not, and yet is.

Babylon is drunk with the blood of the saints and the martyrs of Jesus. The angel is going to reveal the mystery of Babylon and the beast,

who was and is not and who will ascend out of the bottomless pit and go to perdition. Everyone in the world whose names are not in the Book of Life are going to be greatly amazed when they see the beast, who was and is not and yet will be. Since Babylon sits on the beast, and the angel is revealing the mystery of the beast and Babylon together, to understand Babylon we must also have a better understanding of the beast.

REVELATION 17:9-11 (NKJV)
9 "Here is the mind which has wisdom: The seven heads are seven mountains on which the woman sits.
10 There are also seven kings. Five have fallen, one is, and the other has not yet come. And when he comes, he must continue a short time.
11 The beast that was, and is not, is himself also the eighth, and is of the seven, and is going to perdition.

The seven heads are seven mountains. Mountains represent large or global kingdoms. The seven kings are the seven kings, a series of kings, that ruled these great kingdoms. Five have fallen, the sixth one is ruling right now, and the seventh has not yet come, but when comes he will only rule for a short time. The book of the Prophet Daniel has more revelation on Babylon and the beast, and the kingdoms that make up the beast. *Daniel 2* reveals Babylon as a head of gold on a great statue of a man, with the succeeding kingdoms as the next parts on the body of the statue proceeding downward. The chest and arms are silver and is the second kingdom, the stomach and thighs are bronze and is the third kingdom, the legs are iron and is the fourth kingdom, and the feet and toes that are partly of iron and partly of clay is the fifth kingdom. Each succeeding kingdom is made of an inferior metal in terms of wealth, that is kingdom wealth, yet is a stronger metal in terms of strength, which is military strength. Just as iron is able to break and shatter the others into pieces, so the fourth kingdom, which is made of iron, will crush and break all the previous kingdoms into pieces. The fifth kingdom that is a mix of iron and clay will have some of the strength of the iron and some of the weakness and fragility of the clay. Just as iron and clay are different and do not mix, they will not adhere to each other, so this kingdom will have a mix of different people that will not unite with each other and will be divided. *Daniel 7* reveals the first four kingdoms as four different beasts. The first kingdom is Babylon and is a lion with the wings of an eagle, the wings are plucked off and it is made to stand up on two feet like a man and is given the heart of man. The second kingdom is a bear, it is raised up on one side and has three ribs between its teeth. The third kingdom is a leopard with four heads and four wings of a bird. The fourth kingdom is a terrifying and very powerful beast, and with large iron teeth it crushes and devours its victims and tramples underfoot whatever is left. It was different from all the former beasts, and it had ten horns. *Daniel 8* reveals who the second and third kingdoms are; The second kingdom is Media and Persia, and the third kingdom is Greece. From history we know that the kingdom which replaced Greece was the Roman empire, which was known for its great military might and conquests. Babylon, the head of gold, is on top of the statue of a man that represents the current ruling kingdom, which was Babylon at the time, and all the kingdoms that come afterwards, all of which are large kingdoms that ruled many nations, including Babylon. Babylon in the book *Revelation* sits on top of all the kingdoms that came before the current ruling kingdom at the time John wrote the book of *Revelation*, which was Rome, and the kingdoms that come after Rome. As the head of gold, Babylon represents the kingdom with the greatest wealth, and now that we have gained some more understanding of who Babylon is from the book of *Daniel*, it is time to go back to the book of *Revelation* to continue our study of Babylon.

REVELATION 17:15 (NKJV)

[15] Then he said to me, "The waters which you saw, where the harlot sits, are peoples, multitudes, nations, and tongues.

Babylon not only sits on past, present, and future large multinational kingdoms, she also sits on multitudes peoples, nations, and languages.

REVELATION 17:18 (NKJV)

[18] And the woman whom you saw is that great city which reigns over the kings of the earth."

Ancient Babylon was a city and it ruled over the kings of the earth, but that ancient city no longer exists. Nevertheless, Scripture says

that the woman is Babylon and that she is the city that rules over the kings of the earth. The reason Babylon is sitting on top of all these past, present, and future kingdoms that include multitudes of people, nations, and languages is because she rules over them all. This is the mystery of Babylon who the angel revealed rules over all seven of the past, present, and future multinational kingdoms represented by the mountains and many waters she sits on. This can mean only one thing; For Babylon to rule all these past, present, and future kingdoms, she has to be a *spirit*. As a spirit, she could rule through any of these kingdoms at any time. This is the answer to how she is the great city that rules over all the kings of the earth, but also the kingdom that ruled all the other kingdoms. She ruled through the capital city of the kingdom ruling over all the others. As a spirit, in order to rule on the earth, she needs a body. The ruling kingdom and its capital city was the body she used to rule over all the other kingdoms. The beast she sits on and rules through is one body of the past, present, and future kingdoms she rules. The statue in the book of *Daniel* representing the present and future kingdoms ruled by Babylon is one body. The spirit of Babylon's body, the head of the body, is made of gold, which is the kingdom of Babylon. The head sits on top of the body and rules the body, just as Babylon sitting on top of the beast rules all the past, present, and future kingdoms represented by the heads and the body of the beast. Now, the question is how the spirit of Babylon rules over all these kingdoms. The book of *Revelation* has more to reveal about Babylon in *Revelation 18*.

REVELATION 18:1-3 (NKJV)

1 After these things I saw another angel coming down from heaven, having great authority, and the earth was illuminated with his glory.

2 And he cried mightily with a loud voice, saying, "Babylon the great is fallen, is fallen, and has become a dwelling place of demons, a prison for every foul spirit, and a cage for every unclean and hated bird!

3 For all the nations have drunk of the wine of the wrath of her fornication, the kings of the earth have committed fornication with her, and the merchants of the earth have become rich through the abundance of her luxury."

REVELATION 18:9-11 (NKJV)

9 "The kings of the earth who committed fornication and

lived luxuriously with her will weep and lament for her, when they see the smoke of her burning,

[10] standing at a distance for fear of her torment, saying, 'Alas, alas, that great city Babylon, that mighty city! For in one hour your judgment has come.'

[11] "And the merchants of the earth will weep and mourn over her, for no one buys their merchandise anymore:

REVELATION 18:15-19 (NKJV)

[15] The merchants of these things, who became rich by her, will stand at a distance for fear of her torment, weeping and wailing,

[16] and saying, 'Alas, alas, that great city that was clothed in fine linen, purple, and scarlet, and adorned with gold and precious stones and pearls!

[17] For in one hour such great riches came to nothing.' Every shipmaster, all who travel by ship, sailors, and as many as trade on the sea, stood at a distance

[18] and cried out when they saw the smoke of her burning, saying, 'What is like this great city?'

[19] "They threw dust on their heads and cried out, weeping and wailing, and saying, 'Alas, alas, that great city, in which all who had ships on the sea became rich by her wealth! For in one hour she is made desolate.'

Revelation 18 describes the fall and destruction of Babylon, and how that fall has a great impact on many. The great impact of her fall explains how she controls the nations. The merchants became rich by her, the kings of the earth lived luxuriously by her, and when she falls, they cry weeping and wailing because no one buys her merchandise anymore. The passage goes on to say that all who trade by sea also got rich by her, this also means her final place of ruling is located on the seas and not the rivers like ancient Babylon. From *Revelation 18* we can clearly see before she is destroyed Babylon controls much of the wealth and commerce of the world, and with the greatest wealth she would have the greatest influence and control over the nations. Another way she rules over the people we will learn in *Revelation 17*.

REVELATION 17:5 (NKJV)

5 And on her forehead a name was written: MYSTERY, BABYLON THE GREAT, THE MOTHER OF HARLOTS AND OF THE ABOMINATIONS OF THE EARTH.

Through sexual sins and abominations, which causes the people of the world to be led into deeper and deeper darkness. The deeper the darkness that people are led into the blinder they become, and the blinder someone is the easier it is to lead them where you want them to go. In *Revelation 18*, Babylon is called a city repeatedly, further clarifying she is ruling through the capital city of the nation that rules or leads the nations, which is her body. That brings another question— Who destroys Babylon?

REVELATION 17:12,16-17 (NKJV)

12 "The ten horns which you saw are ten kings who have received no kingdom as yet, but they receive authority for one hour as kings with the beast.

16 And the ten horns which you saw on the beast, these will hate the harlot, make her desolate and naked, eat her flesh and burn her with fire.

17 For God has put it into their hearts to fulfill His purpose, to be of one mind, and to give their kingdom to the beast, until the words of God are fulfilled.

These verses say the ten horns on the beast are kings who will not receive a kingdom until the end, and only for one hour, with the beast, will hate Babylon and will destroy her and burn her with fire and eat her flesh. *Verse 17* reveals the One who destroys Babylon; it is God Almighty that puts it into their hearts to destroy Babylon. So, in the end, the beast that Babylon rules through turns on her. The next passage reveals who the final beast is.

REVELATION 17:9-11 (NKJV)

9 "Here is the mind which has wisdom: The seven heads are seven mountains on which the woman sits.

10 There are also seven kings. Five have fallen, one is, and the other has not yet come. And when he comes, he must continue a short time.

¹¹ The beast that was, and is not, is himself also the eighth,
and is of the seven, and is going to perdition.

The final beast is an eighth king. Since the seventh kingdom is the final kingdom that Babylon rules through, and the beast destroys that kingdom, the beast would not be from the seventh kingdom but would come out from one of the kingdoms prior to seventh. This is the fifth kingdom of the statue representing the body of Babylon. That leaves the question—What are the two kingdoms that are not part of the statue that starts with Nebuchadnezzar's Babylon? That Babylon is not the first or even the second kingdom that the spirit of Babylon ruled through. The first city of Babylon is found is *Genesis 11* and was built by Noah's great grandson Nimrod, it is the city known for the famous tower of Babel. Babel is Hebrew for the Greek word Babylon, which both mean "confusion." It was given that name because God came down and confused all the languages to end man's rebellion against His command in *Genesis 1:28* to multiply and fill the earth, to subdue and have dominion over it. Babylon rose again around 2000 BC, and it was the most powerful and wealthiest kingdom on the earth in its time. The most famous king of this empire was king Hammurabi. Babylon did not rise to power again until around 612 BC, this was the Babylon ruled by king Nebuchadnezzar when Daniel the Prophet was carried away as a captive to Babylon. This is the head of gold on the statue given to king Nebuchadnezzar in a dream, which was interpreted by God through Daniel the Prophet. I believe Nimrod's Babylon and Hammurabi's Babylon were the first two kingdoms that were ruled by the spirit of Babylon and were not included in the statue whose gold head is Nebuchadnezzar's Babylon, therefore only representing five kingdoms instead of seven. The beast in *Revelation* shows the spirit of Babylon sitting on all seven kingdoms she has ruled. All three of the cities of Babylon; Nimrod's, Hammurabi's, and Nebuchadnezzar's, were all located in the same location. Today, the location of the ancient cities of Babylon are located in the nation of Iraq. All the kingdoms that the spirit of Babylon has conquered since Nebuchadnezzar's Babylon ruled over the location of the ancient cities of Babylon. The seventh and final kingdom of Babylon would very likely conquer and rule, or at least have some control over, the location of the city of Babylon. That would be the fifth kingdom of the statue in the book of *Daniel*. Let's take another look at that fifth kingdom since it will be the final kingdom ruled by the

spirit of Babylon.

DANIEL 2:41-43 (NIV)

[41] Just as you saw that the feet and toes were partly of baked clay and partly of iron, so this will be a divided kingdom; yet it will have some of the strength of iron in it, even as you saw iron mixed with clay.

[42] As the toes were partly iron and partly clay, so this kingdom will be partly strong and partly brittle.

[43] And just as you saw the iron mixed with baked clay, so the people will be a mixture and will not remain united, any more than iron mixes with clay.

The final kingdom that the spirit of Babylon rules through is symbolized by a mixture of iron and clay, and just as iron and clay cannot unite, this kingdom will not be united and will have division in it even though it is one kingdom. Iron was the metal that symbolized the fourth kingdom of Rome, and its military might. This kingdom will be partly iron and that represents military might, and partly of baked clay, which is brittle and fragile, so this fifth kingdom will be militarily strong but will also be fragile (vulnerable) as well. It will also be a mixture of different people who will not remain united, causing division within this kingdom.

Summary: Who is Babylon the Great?

1. She is a Mystery.
2. Her name is Babylon the Great.
3. She is the mother of prostitutes and the abominations of the earth.
4. She is very decadent and dresses in the richest clothing and jewelry.
5. She has a golden cup in her hand full of abominations and the filthiness of her sexual sins.
6. The rulers of the earth commit sexual sins with her.
7. The people of the world are intoxicated with her sexual sins.
8. She sits on many waters, which is multitudes of peoples, nations, and languages.
9. She sits on the beast with the seven heads and ten horns, the seven heads are seven mountains, which are large multinational kingdoms throughout the ages.

10. She rules the kings of the earth, multitudes of peoples, nations, and languages all throughout the ages.
11. The Mystery of Babylon is that she rules all these large kingdoms, multitudes, nations, and languages throughout the ages.
12. Further explanation of the mystery of Babylon is that she is a spirit that does not die and is able to rise to power over and over again.
13. She rules all these kingdoms by greed and controlling much of the wealth and commerce of the world.
14. She also rules all these kingdoms, peoples, nations, and languages through lust and every kind of sexual sin and abomination, leading them into deeper and deeper darkness where she will have more control over them.
15. Babylon is a city. She started as an ancient city, and she still rules through the capital city of the nation that rules or leads the other nations. The capital city and ruling nation is her body that she rules the kingdoms of the world through.
16. The final kingdom ruled by Babylon is described as part of the statue in *Daniel 2*, the feet and toes made of iron and clay. The iron representing military strength and the clay is weakness and vulnerability. The iron and clay also represent a mix of different peoples and division among the people.
17. The end times Babylon will very likely have rule or control of, for at least some time, the location of the original cities of Babylon, which is currently located in the nation of Iraq.
18. Babylon in the end, like Rome which was the kingdom the spirit of Babylon ruled through during the time of the early Church, will eventually be a great persecutor of the saints. I believe the early Church recognized Rome as the Babylon of their time. The Apostle Peter, while in Rome, gave a greeting from Rome as if he were in Babylon.

REVELATION 17:6 (NKJV)

[6] I saw the woman, drunk with the blood of the saints and with the blood of the martyrs of Jesus. And when I saw her, I marveled with great amazement.

1 PETER 5:13 (NKJV)

[13] She who is in Babylon, elect together with you, greets you; and so does Mark my son.

The very first Babylon, Nimrod's Babylon, was built on man's pride and rebellion symbolized by man trying to build a tower to heaven. Babylon controlling the world's wealth allows her to rule people through greed and being the mother of harlots and abominations. She rules people through the lust of the flesh.

1 JOHN 2:15-16 (NKJV)

¹⁵ Do not love the world or the things in the world. If anyone loves the world, the love of the Father is not in him.
¹⁶ For all that is in the world—the lust of the flesh, the lust of the eyes, and the pride of life—is not of the Father but is of the world.

Babylon is the world, and we are told not to love the lust of the flesh, the lust of the eyes or the pride of life, which are the opposite of the love of God. Remember what Jesus said in *Matthew 24:12-13*.

MATTHEW 24:12-13 (NKJV)

¹² And because lawlessness will abound, the love of many will grow cold.
¹³ But he who endures to the end shall be saved.

If our love grows cold, we will not endure to the end and be saved!

REVELATION 18:4-5 (NKJV)

⁴ And I heard another voice from heaven saying, "Come out of her, my people, lest you share in her sins, and lest you receive of her plagues.
⁵ For her sins have reached to heaven, and God has remembered her iniquities.

The warning to come out of Babylon is very serious. If we do not get out, we will wind up sharing in her sins and sharing her judgment and destruction! So, how do we get out of Babylon? To start with, we need to identify any worldly activity that has sin and stop participating in it. It is easy to identify that we should not go to bars and night clubs, but today, most entertainment is full of all kinds of sins, from different degrees of nudity, sex, language, and excessive bloody violence, there really is very little worldly entertainment in today's culture suitable for God's children. Though many sports in and of themselves are not sinful, many people have turned their favorite sports into an idol and spend far more of their time, energy, and money on them than on God's kingdom. We are going to have to examine our lifestyles and make sure we are not participating in something that is displeasing to God. It can be difficult to find activities in today's culture that do not have sin, but if we spend more of our time seeking and serving God, we will not have as much time for sinful activities. There are wholesome activities, but they are fewer than the many activities that involve sin.

CHAPTER WRAP UP

How can we prepare ourselves for these times? Faith is going to be a key factor, and faith is increased by hearing the Word of God. Spending more time studying, meditating, and applying God's Word, which means to obey Scripture, will increase our faith. Equally as important, we are going to have to listen to God and obey His voice. The more we obey His Word and voice, the more He will speak to us. He said, *"My sheep hear My voice, and I know them, and they follow Me."* Speaking of obeying, He is warning us right now to be prepared to endure and not live by the sword, which means not to fight back but endure the persecution as He did, and as many of the prophets and saints have done. I believe we need to develop this mind and attitude to not fight back before the persecution comes. If we have a mentality to fight back whenever we are attacked, we may be no different when times of persecution comes. Jesus taught His disciples to turn the other cheek, something I am still really trying to fully understand and follow, but I believe Scripture clearly teaches us not to fight back when we are persecuted and in times of persecution. That is another reason for us to understand the times and the signs of the times. We are warned ahead of time not to fight back but to endure the persecution, and we need to take that warning seriously and begin to change our minds and attitudes so that we are not caught off guard and fall when the time of testing comes.

Summarizing the answers to the question of this chapter—*Why is the Truth about the Rapture Important?*

1. Because we need to know the *Whole Truth About the Rapture.*
2. To understand when the Rapture will take place.
3. To not be deceived or ignore the warnings in Scripture.
4. To know to watch for the signs Jesus taught about leading up to the Rapture, which includes the many events of the Great Tribulation and the wrath of God in the first Six Trumpets.
5. To know the time of God's wrath is very serious and that we need to live very obedient lives and walk in the fear of God, like Noah.
6. Knowing when the Rapture takes place, we will know to take all the warnings in Scripture from Jesus and others very seriously.

Because getting sin out of our lives, loving others, and purifying our hearts so our love does not grow cold, that we can be prepared, overcome, and endure to the end.

WHEN IS THE RAPTURE?

PT. 3

THE FOURTH WITNESS

Jesus mentions our fourth witness during His teaching of the Great Tribulation that will occur just before His return for the saints and the Resurrection and Rapture.

MATTHEW 24:15 (NIV)

[15] "So when you see standing in the holy place 'the abomination that causes desolation,' spoken of through the prophet Daniel—let the reader understand—

Jesus mentions the Prophet Daniel when He refers to the *"abomination of desolation."* I stated earlier in this study that the abomination of desolation is the image of the beast, and I gave my reasons for that. The Prophet Daniel describes the abomination of desolation as being set up, and Jesus in all Gospel accounts says, *"when you see standing in the holy place,"* and standing is exactly what you would expect a statue or image to be doing. Paul describes the man of sin, who is the beast and antichrist, sitting on a throne in the temple, and sitting on a throne is what you would expect a ruler to do. Jesus says the setting up of the abomination of desolation causes the Greatest Tribulation in all of history, before or after. So terrible that if He did not shorten those days no flesh would survive, and that is exactly what happens when the image of the beast is setup. The beast will have power and authority over all the nations at that time and anyone who will not worship the image of the beast is executed, causing the worst persecution and Tribulation of the saints ever! Another reason is that the image of the beast is setup during the time of the beast's global rule, which is during the Sixth Trumpet, and the coming of Christ and the Resurrection and Rapture is at the Seventh Trumpet. Jesus says the abomination of desolation is setup right before His coming and the Resurrection and Rapture. I believe this makes for a good case that the abomination of desolation is the image of the beast.

Jesus mentions Daniel because Daniel was the first person God revealed the beast and the abomination of desolation to, and until the book of *Revelation*, God showed Daniel the most that was ever revealed about them. Giving the listener and reader where to learn more about it, Daniel was also given revelation about the Resurrections and the Rapture. I am sure you have figured it out by now, our fourth witness is Daniel the Prophet. Let's see what was revealed to Daniel about the beast and the abomination of desolation and compare it to what John said in the book of *Revelation* and what the Apostle Paul said in his epistles. In *Daniel 7*, the Prophet Daniel is given a vision of four great beasts that represent the kings and kingdoms that would rule the world from his time to the end of time, and out of the fourth beast would come the beast who will rule at the end. Daniel then asked an angelic messenger about the fourth and final beast because it was so terrible. This is what the messenger said to Daniel—

DANIEL 7:23-27 (NKJV)
23 "Thus he said: 'The fourth beast shall be a fourth kingdom on earth, which shall be different from all other kingdoms, and shall devour the whole earth, trample it and break it in pieces.
24 The ten horns are ten kings who shall arise from this kingdom.
And another shall rise after them; he shall be different from the first ones, and shall subdue three kings.
25 He shall speak pompous words against the Most High, shall persecute the saints of the Most High, and shall

intend to change times and law. Then the saints shall be given into his hand for a time and times and half a time.
²⁶ 'But the court shall be seated, and they shall take away his dominion, to consume and destroy it forever.
²⁷ Then the kingdom and dominion, and the greatness of the kingdoms under the whole heaven, shall be given to the people, the saints of the Most High. His kingdom is an everlasting kingdom, and all dominions shall serve and obey Him.'

The fourth beast, which is the Roman empire, devours the whole world, and ten horns, which are kings and kingdoms, will come out of the fourth beast at the end. An eleventh horn shall arise after them and subdue three kings and their kingdoms, and he will speak arrogant and boastful words against God Almighty. The saints, they are given over to his power for a *"time and times and half a time."* A time is a year, so a time and times and half a time are three-and-a-half years. Compare this to what the book of *Revelation* says about the beast.

REVELATION 13:5 (NKJV)
⁵ And he was given a mouth speaking great things and blasphemies, and he was given authority to continue for forty-two months.

The book *Revelation* says the beast speaks blasphemies against God and is given authority to continue for forty-two months. Forty-two months is three-and-a-half years.

REVELATION 13:7-8 (NKJV)
⁷ It was granted to him to make war with the saints and to overcome them. And authority was given him over every tribe, tongue, and nation.
⁸ All who dwell on the earth will worship him, whose names have not been written in the Book of Life of the Lamb slain from the foundation of the world.

So, Daniel and John both say that the beast-antichrist will make war with the saints and overcome them, or as Daniel describes, be given over to his power for three-and-a-half years. I believe, as I said early in this study, the Lord has not only given us the length of time, so we would understand the times, but He used multiple ways of giving the same length of time, three-and-a-half years is forty-two months and forty-two months is one-thousand-two-hundred-and-sixty days. They are all the same measure of time given in multiple ways so they cannot be changed into a different measure of time and yet all still be the same amount of time. God wants us to know that this final global reign of the beast-antichrist will only be three-and-a-half years, and that not only reveals to us how long we have to endure it but also lets us know that the world as we know it is over. This can help us fix our hearts on the Lord and heaven and help us endure no matter what happens during those terrible times.

As we learned in *Revelation 13*, the beast is given authority over all the nations. We also see in *Daniel 7*, this beast character *"He shall speak pompous words against the Most High."* This is similar to what the Apostle Paul said about the man of sin, the antichrist.

2 THESSALONIANS 2:4 (NKJV)
⁴ who opposes and exalts himself above all that is called God or that is worshiped, so that he sits as God in the temple of God, showing himself that he is God.

I believe when the Apostle Paul was describing the man of sin, the son of perdition, he was actually referencing this text and another text we will soon look at that describes the beast in the book of *Daniel*. Let's read more of what Daniel has to say about the beast.

DANIEL 8:23-26 (NKJV)
²³ "And in the latter time of their kingdom, When the transgressors have reached their fullness, A king shall arise, Having fierce features, Who understands sinister schemes.
²⁴ His power shall be mighty, but not by his own power; He shall destroy fearfully, And shall prosper and thrive; He shall destroy the mighty, and also the holy people.
²⁵ "Through his cunning He shall cause deceit to prosper under his rule; And he shall exalt himself in his heart. He shall destroy many in their prosperity. He shall even rise against the Prince of princes; But he shall be broken without human means.

²⁶ "And the vision of the evenings and mornings Which was told is true; Therefore seal up the vision, For it refers to many days in the future."

The Angel Gabriel is the one describing this to Daniel, and the first thing he says is this; *"And in the latter time of their kingdom, when the transgressors have reached their fullness,"* meaning the sinful and wicked people will have reached full maturity in their wickedness and will be very wicked, just like the times of Noah, and Sodom and Gomorrah. Jesus taught, before He returns, it would be like the days of Noah and Sodom and Gomorrah. He also said that it would be a time of harvest, and the tares, the sons of the devil, would reach full maturity, and the wheat, the sons of God, would also reach full maturity and you would be able to easily distinguish them from each other. Gabriel tells Daniel that he will destroy the mighty and the holy people, this agrees with and confirms what we have learned from *Daniel 7* and *Revelation 13,* the beast wages war against the saints for three-and-a-half years. He says this king will have a fierce appearance and will be a sinister person who causes deceit to prosper, meaning there is going to be great deception everywhere. *Revelation 13:8* reveals how great that deception will be, *"All who dwell on the earth will worship him, whose names have not been written in the Book of Life of the Lamb slain from the foundation of the world."* This character is going to have everyone who is not written in the Lamb's Book of Life so deceived that they are going to believe he is god, and they will worship him. If they believe he is god, what else will they be willing to do for him aside from worshiping him? Most likely anything, including killing anyone who opposes him. The next thing Gabriel tells Daniel is he will rise against the Prince of princes and be broken without human means. The Prince of princes is Jesus Christ, and He destroys the beast with the power of God, not human weapons. Now let's read what the book of *Revelation* says about that.

REVELATION 19:11 (NKJV)
¹¹ Now I saw heaven opened, and behold, a white horse.
And He who sat on him was called Faithful and True, and
in righteousness He judges and makes war.

This is a description of the Lord Jesus Christ on a white horse coming to earth to make war with the beast and take back the earth.

REVELATION 19:19-20 (NKJV)

19 And I saw the beast, the kings of the earth, and their armies, gathered together to make war against Him who sat on the horse and against His army.

20 Then the beast was captured, and with him the false prophet who worked signs in his presence, by which he deceived those who received the mark of the beast and those who worshiped his image. These two were cast alive into the lake of fire burning with brimstone.

Here we see the beast gathering a global army against the Prince of princes, Jesus Christ, just like it says in the book of Daniel. As we can see, Daniel was given quite a bit of information about the end times and the beast, and it agrees with what the book of *Revelation* says. Even though the book of *Revelation* expands on what was revealed to Daniel, Daniel was given some knowledge that holds the keys to fully understanding the book of *Revelation*. Finally, Gabriel tells Daniel to seal up his vision because it pertains to a generation far in the future. Daniel's generation and many generations after would not really need to understand it, but the last generation will need to understand it.

DANIEL 9:27 (NKJV)

27 He will confirm a covenant with many for one 'seven.' In the middle of the 'seven' he will put an end to sacrifice and offering. And at the temple he will set up an abomination that causes desolation, until the end that is decreed is poured out on him."

Scripture says the beast will confirm a covenant with many for one "seven." The many is the people of Israel and the one seven is a seven-year period, a seven-year period of seventy, seven-year periods for the people of Israel and their holy city Jerusalem. This is described in the previous verses in this passage, *verses 24-26*. This covenant is also called a holy covenant, because the covenant he establishes with them was to allow them to have control of the holy temple and make the holy sacrifices to God in the holy place as prescribed in the Torah, the Old Testament. But then, the beast, sometime in the middle of the seven-year period, puts an end to the sacrifice and offering in the temple, and

after that, sometime later, he sets up the abomination of desolation, which Jesus taught would cause the Greatest Tribulation of all time right before His coming and the Resurrection and Rapture, up until the decree against him is poured out. *Revelation 16* is where the seven bowl judgements of the Seventh Trumpet is poured out on the beast and his kingdom.

DANIEL 11:31 (NKJV)

³¹ And forces shall be mustered by him, and they shall defile the sanctuary fortress; then they shall take away the daily sacrifices, and place there the abomination of desolation.

The beast raises up forces and takes over the sanctuary, which is God's temple. After taking over the temple by force, he takes away the daily sacrifices, and afterward he sets up the abomination of desolation in the holy place, which is where the sacrifices are made. As we have learned from *Revelation 13*, the abomination of desolation is the image of this evil beast, and through satanic power will appear to be alive. As we will see next, it is revealed to Daniel in *Daniel 12* that there is a gap of time between the taking away of the daily sacrifices and the setting up of the abomination of desolation. Let's continue this passage because there is more that is revealed about the beast and the saints here.

DANIEL 11:32-33 (NKJV)

³² Those who do wickedly against the covenant he shall corrupt with flattery; but the people who know their God shall be strong, and carry out great exploits.
³³ And those of the people who understand shall instruct many; yet for many days they shall fall by sword and flame, by captivity and plundering.

The beast will corrupt with his flattery those who work to destroy the covenant. This is a time of tribulation, but also an opportunity for the holy saints during this time. Those who truly know God will carry out great exploits, meaning they will be performing miraculous signs and wonders in the name of Jesus Christ and the power of God's Holy Spirit. Jesus said in Scripture that some would do greater works than He did, and I believe this will be that time. The Tribulation will very difficult times, many saints are to be killed by the sword and fire, some will be imprisoned, and many, if not most, will be plundered (have all their possessions taken away), this will include basic needs like food and clothing. It will be a time when the saints will have to trust the Lord more than ever for all their needs. I want to add a note here; As I have written this book, I have included Scriptures that the Lord has given us to help us prepare for these times, and I want to add a couple Scriptures and a few words here to help us prepare. The Lord has given many promises to those who truly help the poor, including that they will never have to beg for food. Here is just one passage of such promises.

PSALM 37:25-26 (NKJV)

25 I have been young, and now am old; Yet I have not seen the righteous forsaken, Nor his descendants begging bread.
26 He is ever merciful, and lends; And his descendants are blessed.

We are taught by our Lord Jesus Christ in all four Gospels to be generous to the poor, and if we will obey these teachings, we can expect the Lord to keep His promises. We may suffer, but as we learned, our suffering is for His glory and our glory, and when we truly need something, He will provide it. But we must also remember to pray for it.

DANIEL 11:34-35 (NKJV)

34 Now when they fall, they shall be aided with a little help; but many shall join with them by intrigue.
35 And some of those of understanding shall fall, to refine them, purify them, and make them white, until the time of the end; because it is still for the appointed time.

These verses say that the saints will receive a little help, and I believe this is referring to human help, but many will join by intrigue, and intrigue has two meanings that I believe both apply here. Since some of the saints who truly know God are going to be performing signs and miracles, many are going to be joining just because of a strong interest (intrigue) in the signs and miracles. I believe some of them will not be sincere and have divisive plans, the other meaning of the word intrigue. Jesus taught us this would happen during the Tribulation in *Matthew 24*.

MATTHEW 24:10 (NKJV)
¹⁰ And then many will be offended, will betray one another, and will hate one another.

Verse 35 says many of understanding, the ones who understand the times and will be instructing many as stated in *verses 32 and 33,* will fall in order to refine, purify and make like white the bride of Christ. As we have learned, the Lord is coming back for a pure and spotless bride, and it should be expected that some of the saints will fall. I believe the fall, on one hand, is to bring some into further repentance needed to purify their souls, and on the other hand, to purify the insincere from the saints. The Apostle Paul taught about the falling away of believers in *2 Thessalonians 2*, and the later it gets, like the ten virgins, the more likely a fall will be a falling away. This is the Tribulation of the saints and the dark night of the ten virgins, so this will be very late. We need to always walk in the fear of God. Speaking of the fear of God, *verses 32 and 33* are referring to the instructors who understand the times, probably some of whom are performing miracles when they fall, and it says they know their God!

DANIEL 11:36-37 (NKJV)
³⁶ "Then the king shall do according to his own will: he shall exalt and magnify himself above every god, shall speak blasphemies against the God of gods, and shall prosper till the wrath has been accomplished; for what has been determined shall be done.
³⁷ He shall regard neither the God of his fathers nor the desire of women, nor regard any god; for he shall exalt himself above them all.

Reviewing what Daniel says in *Daniel 7*.

DANIEL 7:25 (NKJV)
²⁵ He shall speak pompous words against the Most High, shall persecute the saints of the Most High

You can see here why I said Paul was referencing Daniel when he wrote about the man of sin, the son of perdition who is the beast and the antichrist, who comes before the Rapture. As you can see, Daniel was the first to write about the falling away that the Apostle Paul also wrote about in the same passages he wrote about the antichrist. This is not surprising since Jesus often quoted Scripture and then expounded on it. I believe Paul was doing the same thing. Here is Paul's description in *verse 4*.

2 THESSALONIANS 2:4 (NKJV)

⁴ who opposes and exalts himself above all that is called God or that is worshiped, so that he sits as God in the temple of God, showing himself that he is God.

We know from many passages we have studied that the temple is the center stage to what the antichrist is doing, and that he takes it over and speaks blasphemies against the one true God and demands to be worshiped as god. Paul expounds on this further and explains that the beast-antichrist goes as far as to actually set up a throne in the temple and sits on it opposing the one true God, claiming that he is god.

One last thing I want to cover is in *Daniel 11:36, it* says *"and shall prosper till the wrath has been accomplished."* The beast will be prosperous, in other words he will be successful, until the wrath is accomplished, which means completed. We have learned from *Revelation 15* that it reveals the wrath of God is completed with the seven last plagues, which are the seven bowl judgements that are poured out on the beast, destroying his kingdom.

REVELATION 15:1 (NKJV)

¹ Then I saw another sign in heaven, great and marvelous: seven angels having the seven last plagues, for in them the wrath of God is complete.

As you can see, the teachings of the Apostle Paul, John in the book and *Revelation* and Jesus in the Gospels, many of their teachings on this subject are directly related to the teachings in the book of *Daniel,* and they go on to expound and give further revelations. But there are some more revelations in the book of *Daniel* where there are some important details not found in the New Testament, and one of those is the times. Though all the teachings on the times collaborate between *Daniel* and the New Testament, there are some specific details in the book of *Daniel* that are not in the New Testament.

DANIEL 12:4 (NKJV)

4 "But you, Daniel, shut up the words, and seal the book until the time of the end; many shall run to and fro, and knowledge shall increase."

Daniel is told to seal up the book until the time of the end, and he is told again.

DANIEL 12:9 (NKJV)

9 And he said, "Go your way, Daniel, for the words are closed up and sealed till the time of the end.

Daniel is told to seal up what he is shown until the time of the end. What is the time of the end? It is a period of time at the end. What is that end? It is what we have been studying, the end of man's rule on the earth with the final ruler being the beast, who is the antichrist. After this, the One True Christ will come and rule the earth forever. Daniel was told to seal up what he was shown about the future three distinct times. The first time was in *Daniel 8*.

DANIEL 8:26 (NKJV)

26 "And the vision of the evenings and mornings Which was told is true; Therefore seal up the vision, For it refers to many days in the future."

Here, Daniel is told to seal his vision up because it refers to many days in the future, meaning far into the future. Why seal up a vision for a time far in the future? Because Daniel's generation and many generations to come would not need to understand this vision. But why give it the first place? Because there would come a final generation that would need to understand this vision. Those seeking the truth in that generation will be given understanding of the vision he was told to seal up.

DANIEL 12:5-7 (NKJV)

5 Then I, Daniel, looked; and there stood two others, one on this riverbank and the other on that riverbank.

⁶ And one said to the man clothed in linen, who was above the waters of the river, "How long shall the fulfillment of these wonders be?"
⁷ Then I heard the man clothed in linen, who was above the waters of the river, when he held up his right hand and his left hand to heaven, and swore by Him who lives forever, that it shall be for a time, times, and half a time; and when the power of the holy people has been completely shattered, all these things shall be finished.

DANIEL 7:25 (NKJV)
²⁵ He shall speak pompous words against the Most High, shall persecute the saints of the Most High, and shall intend to change times and law. Then the saints shall be given into his hand for a time and times and half a time.

Comparing these verses, twice Daniel is told that the holy people, who are the saints, will suffer severe persecution under the beast for three-and-a-half years, and they are given over to the persecution of the beast until their power to fight back is completely shattered. We know the saints will have some power to fight because it says until their power is completely shattered, they will do great works and miracles.

REVELATION 13:7 (NKJV)
⁷ It was granted to him to make war with the saints and to overcome them. And authority was given him over every tribe, tongue, and nation.

The beast is granted forty-two months to make war with the saints, suggesting the saints did have some power to fight back against the beasts, but twice we are told that the beast will overcome the saints. Question—What kind of war do the saints wage? *Revelation 13,* the chapter that gives detailed descriptions of the beast.

REVELATION 13:9-10 (NKJV)
⁹ If anyone has an ear, let him hear.
¹⁰ He who leads into captivity shall go into captivity; he who kills with the sword must be killed with the sword. Here is the patience and the faith of the saints.

The Lord is saying here that it is the patience and faith of the saints that allows them to endure the persecution of the beast. The apostles and early saints suffered severe persecution and death also, and they endured it and overcame it by continuing to preach the Gospel, heal the sick and perform other miracles. There may be some who take up arms against the beast in disobedience to the Lord's command in *Revelation 13:10*, but they will not prevail but rather die by the sword in disobedience to the Lord.

DANIEL 11:32-33 (NKJV)
32 Those who do wickedly against the covenant he shall corrupt with flattery; but the people who know their God shall be strong, and carry out great exploits.
33 And those of the people who understand shall instruct many; yet for many days they shall fall by sword and flame, by captivity and plundering.

I believe the saints who keep the faith will wage war against the beast in the same way the apostles and early saints did, and that is exactly what the book Daniel says they will do. They will instruct many in the word about the Lord through preaching and teaching and do great exploits (miracles), and just like the early saints they will be martyred for it. But by waging war this way they will help many endure to the end of these horrible times and not be lost to the falling away.

DANIEL 12:8-10 (NKJV)
8 Although I heard, I did not understand. Then I said, "My lord, what shall be the end of these things?"
9 And he said, "Go your way, Daniel, for the words are closed up and sealed till the time of the end.
10 Many shall be purified, made white, and refined, but the wicked shall do wickedly; and none of the wicked shall understand, but the wise shall understand.

It will be exactly as it says here, the wicked will not understand what has happened to the world. They will be completely given over to evil and will accept the beast as their ruler, their hero and savior, and they will worship him as god. But the wise will understand what is happening to the world, that the global ruler who thinks he is god is not the Messiah but the antichrist who will be at war against all true followers of the Living God and His Christ. Because the world at large has become completely wicked like the days of Noah and Sodom and Gomorrah, it is now experiencing the judgement and wrath of God on a semi-global scale as prophesied in Scripture, especially in the book of *Revelation*. The wise will also understand the times and signs of the times and will be prepared to endure the long dark night of the ten virgins waiting for their Bridegroom—their Lord and Savior Jesus Christ. As recently stated, the book of *Daniel* has details concerning the times no other book in the Bible has. Daniel was told to seal them up because understanding this revelation would not be needed until far in the future, at the time of the end. These details concerning the time of the end in the book of *Daniel* also gives details concerning the timing of the Rapture, which I believe the saints of the last days will need to know. The verses in *Daniel 12* will reveal these times. Before we read these verses, I want to read *Daniel 9:27* again.

DANIEL 9:27 (NKJV)
²⁷ He will confirm a covenant with many for one 'seven.' In the middle of the 'seven' he will put an end to sacrifice and offering. And at the temple he will set up an abomination that causes desolation, until the end that is decreed is poured out on him."

As we have learned earlier in this chapter, the one seven is the last seven-year period of seventy, seven-year periods for Israel and Jerusalem. It says in the middle of the seven, he, the beast, will put an end to sacrifice and offerings. I believe that Scripture says *"In the middle"* here instead of one-thousand-two-hundred-and-sixty days, or forty-two months, or even three-and-a-half years, because all of which are exactly half of seven years, as it says in all other places in Scripture. By using the word "middle" instead of the exact number of days, months, or years, it can be approximately three-and-a-half years and not have to be interpreted as three-and-a-half years into the seven-year period. I truly believe this is the case, and you will know why next.

DANIEL 12:11-13 (NKJV)
¹¹ "And from the time that the daily sacrifice is taken away, and the abomination of desolation is set up, there shall be one thousand two hundred and ninety days.

¹² Blessed is he who waits, and comes to the one thousand three hundred and thirty-five days.
¹³ "But you, go your way till the end; for you shall rest, and will arise to your inheritance at the end of the days."

We just read in *Daniel 9:27* that the daily sacrifice is taken away in the middle, approximately three-and-a-half years of the last seven years, and now we see Scripture says the abomination of desolation is set up one-thousand-two-hundred-and-ninety days, which is also approximately three-and-a-half years. If the daily sacrifice is taken away in middle of the seven years, and the abomination of desolation is setup approximately three-and-a-half years later, this means the abomination of desolation is setup near the end of the seven-year period. The next verse in the book of *Daniel* says, *"Blessed is he who waits, and comes to the one thousand three hundred and thirty-five days." Verse 11* says the daily sacrifice is taken away about halfway through the seven-year period, and then one-thousand-two-hundred-and-ninety days later the abomination of desolation, which is the image of the beast, is set up. Then so, Scripture says blessed are those who make it to the one-thousand-three-hundred-and-thirty-five days, which is forty-five days after the abomination of desolation is set up and is still approximately three-and-a-half years after the daily sacrifice is taken away. Reviewing what Jesus said in *Matthew 24*.

MATTHEW 24:15, 21-22 (NKJV)
¹⁵ "Therefore when you see the 'abomination of desolation,' spoken of by Daniel the prophet, standing in the holy place" (whoever reads, let him understand),
²¹ For then there will be great tribulation, such as has not been since the beginning of the world until this time, no, nor ever shall be.
²² And unless those days were shortened, no flesh would be saved; but for the elect's sake those days will be shortened.

Jesus is clearly saying here that this will be the Greatest Tribulation in the history of the world, before or after. It will be so great that if he does not shorten those days no flesh would be saved. This explains why the time is only forty-five days. The beast will have full global authority and power at that time and will have been waging war against the saints for almost three-and-a-half years, and has overcome them, and has probably reached a point where he can no longer force the saints still alive to take his mark. So, he sets up and satanically powered, life like image of the beast and is going kill anyone who does not worship his image. It is going to be a worldwide execution of anyone who will not bow down and worship this statue that appears by satanic power to be alive. Remember, it only took forty days for a global rain to kill every human and animal on earth, with global power and control the beast would be able to kill anyone and everyone he wants to.

Jesus says, *"no flesh would be saved,"* yet we know the beast is not going to kill everyone who has the mark of the beast and is devoted to him, only those who will not worship his image. So how is it that no fleshed will be saved? Remember in *Revelation 11*, we learned the beast's reign is during the Sixth Trumpet, and Jesus returns to Judge the earth shortly after at the Seventh Trumpet. If the Lord did not shorten the time, the beast would have time to kill everyone who will not worship his image, leaving only the people who worship the beast and his image and have his mark. Then at the Seventh Trumpet when Jesus returns, He will kill and execute everyone who has the mark of the beast, literally leaving no human being in the flesh left alive on the earth. As we read in the second part of *verse 12*, blessed is he who makes it to the one-thousand-three-hundred-and-thirty-fifth day, which is forty-five days after the abomination of desolation is set up. What are the saints waiting for, for forty-five days after the image of the beast is setup? I believe the answer is obvious, they are waiting for the Lord to rescue them from the beast. In other words, they are waiting for the coming of the Lord in the sky at Seventh and Last Trumpet, the Rapture of those who are still alive and remain and have not been killed by the beast. Now that we have studied the details about the times found only in the book of *Daniel,* and by God's Grace, I believe we have unraveled the meaning of one very important time. We have learned that the Rapture is forty-five days after the setting up of the abomination of desolation, the image of the beast. So, the answer to the question of this chapter— *When is the Rapture?* It is forty-five days after the setting up of the abomination of desolation.

The good news for those who live through these times is that the wise will understand the Scriptures and the times, and they will know

that they only have to endure the most terrible time in all of human history for forty-five days. Then they will be with the Lord forever instead of soon facing eternal doom and damnation in the lake of fire with those who take the mark of the beast. This may not seem like a great thing for someone who is not going through it, but for those still alive at the time of the Great Tribulation, knowing when it is going to come to an end and that it is not going to be a long time, I believe will be a great encouragement to them and actually help them endure, which is why the Lord gave them the times to begin with.

Jesus said no one knows the day or hour, but he did say we could understand the times by the signs of the times. The taking away of the daily sacrifice and the abomination of desolation are signs of the times. Daniel was told to seal this up because these events (signs) were far in the future, so no one in Daniel's time could ever know the day or hour. No one in Jesus time could know because it was still far in the future. In fact, no generation will know until these events take place, then those who know Scripture will be able to know the day because they will need to know it to help them endure to the end. They will not know the day until the daily sacrifice is taken away, then it will be one-thousand-two-hundred-and-ninety days from that time until the abomination of desolation of is setup, and one-thousand-three-hundred-and-thirty-five days until the Lord comes and Raptures the saints still alive. After the daily sacrifice is taken away some time in the middle of the seven years, and this will also be the approximate time the beast will begin his three-and-a-half-year global reign, we know this three-and-a-half years will be a Great Tribulation because the beast will be making war with the saints and severely persecuting them. War is one thing, but an all-out execution is another. When the image of the beast, the abomination of desolation, is set up, it will start the greatest and most terrible Tribulation ever, so terrible it can only be allowed to last forty-five days or else everyone not devoted to the beast will be wiped out! So, to restate this and help make it clear, no one will know the time of the Rapture until the daily sacrifice is taken away, then the Rapture will be one-thousand-three-hundred-and-thirty-five days later, and just before the Rapture, one-thousand-two-hundred-and-ninety days after the daily sacrifice is taken away, the image of the beast, the abomination of desolation, is set up, which is forty-five days before the Rapture. As I have stated and truly believe, the people living through these times will need to understand the times. They will know the day of the Rapture if they truly know the Scriptures.

The Lord in Scripture has often told people how long they would have to endure and suffer. One example is the seventy years in Babylon, and another specially, to the people who would be martyred in the book of *Revelation*.

REVELATION 2:10 (NKJV)

[10] Do not fear any of those things which you are about to suffer. Indeed, the devil is about to throw some of you into prison, that you may be tested, and you will have tribulation ten days. Be faithful until death, and I will give you the crown of life.

Here the Lord is speaking to the Church of Ephesus. The first thing He says is *"Do not fear"* what you are about to suffer. What words of encouragement did He give them to help them not to fear? The most important is the eternal reward of a crown, which represents authority, specifically the crown of life. The next encouragement He gave is that the Tribulation is a test, and that it would only last ten days. This is no little encouragement if you know you are going be tested with tribulation to the point of death, but knowing how long it is going to last is very important. If the Lord had not told them how long it would last, they may have been overwhelmed thinking it would last forever and possibly give up and deny the Lord and lose the crown of life, and possibly, their eternal life. The final Greatest Tribulation may very well be too much to endure if the saints do not know how long it will last, but the Lord has provided this in Scripture and He is unraveling the mystery for the final generations that will have to endure these times.

QUESTION 10

WHAT HAPPENS AFTER THE RAPTURE?

Now we are at the tenth and final question—*What happens after the Rapture?* I have included this question because there will be very important events happening after the Rapture that we need to understand to see the whole picture that Scripture paints concerning the Rapture.

We know the Rapture happens after the Tribulation and the Resurrection, after the dead in Christ are raised and at the Last Trumpet of God, which is the Seventh and Last Trumpet of God in the book of Revelation. We also learned the completion of God's wrath comes at the Seventh Trumpet in the pouring out of the Seven Bowl Judgements, also called the Third Woe, which is worse than all Six Trumpets combined. Since both of these come at the Last Trumpet, it gives us a question—Does Scripture show that the Resurrection and Rapture come before the Bowl Judgments? Yes, it does. Let's examine the passages that confirm this.

MATTHEW 24:29-31 (NKJV)

29 "Immediately after the tribulation of those days the sun will be darkened, and the moon will not give its light; the stars will fall from heaven, and the powers of the heavens will be shaken.

30 Then the sign of the Son of Man will appear in heaven, and then all the tribes of the earth will mourn, and they will see the Son of Man coming on the clouds of heaven with power and great glory

31 AND HE WILL SEND HIS ANGELS WITH A GREAT SOUND OF A TRUMPET, and they will gather together His elect from the four winds, from one end of heaven to the other.

He sends His angels to gather His people with the sound of a trumpet. That means they are sent, literally, when the trumpet sounds. We know this is the Last Trumpet because the Resurrection and Rapture are at the Last Trumpet. Let's look at the Rapture verses in *1 Corinthians 15:51-52* which actually states, *"the last trumpet."*

I CORINTHIANS 15:51-52 (NKJV)

51 Behold, I tell you a mystery: We shall not all sleep, but we shall all be changed—
52 in a moment, in the twinkling of an eye, at the last trumpet. For the trumpet will sound, and the dead will be raised incorruptible, and we shall be changed.

"In a moment, in the twinkling of an eye, at the last trumpet. For the trumpet will sound, and the dead will be raised." This makes it clear that the Resurrection, immediately followed by the Rapture, happens right at the sounding of the Last Trumpet, and the saints will be with Christ when the Bowl Judgements begin to be poured out on the whole earth.

Revelation 15:1-3 reveals that we are with Christ when the bowls are poured out. Before we look at that, I want to look at the pre-Great-Tribulation martyrs who are already in heaven, found in *Revelation 6.*

REVELATION 6:9-11 (NKJV)

9 When He opened the Fifth Seal, I saw under the altar the souls of those who had been slain for the word of God and for the testimony which they held.
10 And they cried with a loud voice, saying, "How long, O Lord, holy and true, until You judge and avenge our blood on those who dwell on the earth?"
11 Then a white robe was given to each of them; and it was said to them that they should rest a little while longer, until both the number of their fellow servants and their

brethren, who would be killed as they were, was completed.

When the Fifth Seal is released, John is given a vision of the saints who have been martyred throughout the ages for the word of God, they are under the alter crying out to God asking Him to judge the wicked and avenge their blood. They are given white robes and are told to rest a little longer until the rest of the saints that will be martyred is complete. The Lord is telling them that they have to wait for Him to avenge their blood until all the saints that are going to be martyred are killed. Why is that? I believe the answer is in *Revelation 15*.

REVELATION 15:1-3 (NKJV)

¹ Then I saw another sign in heaven, great and marvelous: seven angels having the seven last plagues, for in them the wrath of God is complete.
² And I saw something like a sea of glass mingled with fire, and those who have the victory over the beast, over his image and over his mark and over the number of his name, standing on the sea of glass, having harps of God.
³ They sing the song of Moses, the servant of God, and the song of the Lamb, saying: "Great and marvelous are Your works,
Lord God Almighty!
Just and true are Your ways, O King of the saints!

Here, the Seven Bowls are preparing to be poured out on the earth. We see the martyrs after the Great Tribulation, the time of the beast and his mark, standing on this sea of glass singing and they are joyful instead of under the alter crying out for vengeance of their blood. What is the difference? For one, the Bowl Judgments are getting ready to be poured out. Let's look at the three bowls again and we will understand.

REVELATION 16:1-7 (NKJV)

¹ Then I heard a loud voice from the temple saying to the seven angels, "Go and pour out the bowls of the wrath of God on the earth." First

² So the first went and poured out his bowl upon the earth, and a foul and loathsome sore came upon the men who had the mark of the beast and those who worshiped his image.
³ Then the second angel poured out his bowl on the sea, and it became blood as of a dead man; and every living creature in the sea died.
⁴ Then the third angel poured out his bowl on the rivers and springs of water, and they became blood.
⁵ And I heard the angel of the waters saying:" You are righteous, O Lord, The One who is and who was and who is to be, Because You have judged these things.
⁶ For they have shed the blood of saints and prophets, And You have given them blood to drink. For it is their just due."
⁷ And I heard another from the altar saying, "Even so, Lord God Almighty, true and righteous are Your judgments."

Remember, during the Fifth Seal the martyrs were crying out for their blood to be avenged, the Lord told them to wait until all those who were going to be martyred was complete. Now, all the martyrs are in heaven watching the bowls of God's judgment being poured out on the earth against the beast and his worshipers. The third bowl judgment is specifically said to be a judgement against those who have shed the blood of God's saints and prophets. This judgement is to turn all the water in the world to blood so that they have no water to drink and have to drink blood. The Bowl Judgements are poured out after the Seventh Trumpet, the Resurrection and Rapture, and the judgement of rewarding the saints. For the martyrs to watch the bowls being poured out from heaven after the Seventh Trumpet, the Resurrection must have happened right at the sounding of the Seventh Trumpet, just as the Scripture says. This judgement is, at least in part, for the martyrs since the Lord said He would avenge their blood. It would make perfect sense for them to witness this judgement from a place where they can see everything that is happening, and the one place where everything that is happening on the earth can be seen is God's throne.

I believe this provides sufficient evidence that the saints are Resurrected and Raptured before the start of the Bowl Judgements and will witness these judgements poured out on the earth. Now let's look

at the rest of the bowl judgments.

REVELATION 16:8-9 (NKJV)

8 Then the fourth angel poured out his bowl on the sun, and power was given to him to scorch men with fire.
9 And men were scorched with great heat, and they blasphemed the name of God who has power over these plagues; and they did not repent and give Him glory.

Notice that the people on the earth know that it is God who is pouring out these judgments, and instead of fearing Him and repenting, they curse Him.

REVELATION 16:10-11 (NKJV)

10 Then the fifth angel poured out his bowl on the throne of the beast, and his kingdom became full of darkness; and they gnawed their tongues because of the pain.
11 They blasphemed the God of heaven because of their pains and their sores, and did not repent of their deeds.

Again, this verse makes it clear that they know this is God's judgement, and again, instead of fearing Him and repenting, they continue to blaspheme Him. It is highly likely most of the people left on the earth have taken the mark of the beast and are part of his kingdom. If you remember in *Revelation 13,* there is no forgiveness for those who have taken the mark of the beast. Like Pharaoh when God brought judgement against him and Egypt in *Exodus 7-11,* God hardened Pharaoh's heart so he could not repent. These people, like Pharaoh, their hearts have been hardened so they cannot repent. Scripture says in *Hebrews 9:27, "it is appointed for men to die once, but after this the judgment."* But like Pharaoh, sometimes those still alive suffer God's wrath on the earth and have been judged before they die. Not only can someone die at any time and come into judgment, but we also need to fear God and repent while there is still time, not knowing when God will bring His wrath and judgement on the living where He can and will harden the hearts of those whom He is judging.

REVELATION 16:12-14,16 (NKJV)

¹² Then the sixth angel poured out his bowl on the great river Euphrates, and its water was dried up, so that the way of the kings from the east might be prepared.

¹³ And I saw three unclean spirits like frogs coming out of the mouth of the dragon, out of the mouth of the beast, and out of the mouth of the false prophet.

¹⁴ For they are spirits of demons, performing signs, which go out to the kings of the earth and of the whole world, to gather them to the battle of that great day of God Almighty.

¹⁶ And they gathered them together to the place called in Hebrew, Armageddon.

The sixth bowl is poured out on the Euphrates River to dry it up and make way so the armies of the east can gather together to battle with Christ at His return. Demons come out of the beast, the false prophet and the dragon, the same demons who performed signs for the beast and the false prophet, to gather all the armies of the world to fight against Christ in the final battle of the age at a place called Armageddon, which is in Israel. In Hebrew, Armageddon is pronounced Har Megiddo *(Tel Megiddo)*. With only one more bowl to be poured out, and all the world gathering for the battle of Armageddon, the Lord's return to the earth with us is very soon. Before we look at the seventh and last bowl, I want to show you something that I believe is happening during the time the Bowl Judgments are being poured out. We know from the request of the martyrs seen in the vision of the Fifth Seal, and the martyrs in *Revelation 15* celebrating before God's throne, the martyrs are very likely witnessing what is happening on the earth when the Bowl Judgements are being poured out. We also know that there is a wedding soon after the Resurrection and Rapture, and judgement of the saints. How big do you think that wedding table will be with millions, maybe even billions, of saints sitting together with angels attending?

PSALM 23:5 (NKJV)

⁵ You prepare a table before me in the presence of my enemies;
You anoint my head with oil; My cup runs over.

I believe this verse's ultimate fulfillment is during the Marriage

Supper of the Lamb. What fulfills this verse is not the saints watching the judgment of the wicked, and those who tormented them now watching the saints in heaven sitting at the most glorious table ever. Instead, set before the saints in the presence of their enemies, the wicked have nothing but blood to drink, the only food left is human flesh and what is left of their kingdom is being completely destroyed. Seeing the saints that they hated so much now sitting in glory would make suffering their judgment that much worse. I believe the following passages give further evidence of this.

REVELATION 6:14-17 (NKJV)

14 Then the sky receded as a scroll when it is rolled up, and every mountain and island was moved out of its place.
15 And the kings of the earth, the great men, the rich men, the commanders, the mighty men, every slave and every free man, hid themselves in the caves and in the rocks of the mountains,
16 and said to the mountains and rocks, "Fall on us and hide us from the face of Him who sits on the throne and from the wrath of the Lamb!
17 For the great day of His wrath has come, and who is able to stand?"

These verses say that the sky recedes and rolls up like a scroll, they see God Almighty sitting on His throne with Christ. I believe this is the Seventh Trumpet, and the people of the earth are not only going to see Christ coming but the veil between heaven and earth has been rolled back. They are seeing into heaven and see God sitting on His throne. The people of the earth know God's wrath is going to be poured out on them soon and everyone is desperately trying to hide from the wrath of God and Christ. They are so desperate that they are asking the mountains to fall on them and hide them from God's wrath. The sixth bowl says the armies of the earth are gathering together to fight a war with Christ. Most of the Bowl Judgements have been poured out and the people of the earth realize hiding is not going to save them from God's wrath. They now do the only thing they can do to try and save themselves; they prepare for a global war with Christ. They are very likely seeing Christ preparing to come back and make war with them, and that means the veil between heaven and earth is still rolled back.

The people of the earth are seeing into heaven and see what they have lost, and they have already seen their enemies at the most glorious table ever set, feasting while they receive their judgement of doom. Now all they can do is follow their false god into battle with the One True God, and falsely hope their god is the real God.

THE SEVENTH AND FINAL BOWL JUDGEMENT

REVELATION 16:17-21 (NKJV)

[17] Then the seventh angel poured out his bowl into the air, and a loud voice came out of the temple of heaven, from the throne, saying, "It is done!"

[18] And there were noises and thundering's and lightnings; and there was a great earthquake, such a mighty and great earthquake as had not occurred since men were on the earth.

[19] Now the great city was divided into three parts, and the cities of the nation's fell. And great Babylon was remembered before God, to give her the cup of the wine of the fierceness of His wrath.

[20] Then every island fled away, and the mountains were not found.

[21] And great hail from heaven fell upon men, each hailstone about the weight of a talent. Men blasphemed God because of the plague of the hail, since that plague was exceedingly great.

God finishes His wrath with the seventh bowl, and with it He causes the worst earthquake in all of human history destroying all the cities of the earth, which is going to bring down most, if not all, the tall buildings and high towers, which are symbols of man's pride and achievements. God says He remembered Babylon the great in the outpouring of His wrath. It is hard to image an earthquake so great that the islands and mountains disappear, but that is what Scripture says and we can believe it. Then a great hailstorm with one-hundred-pound hailstones falls on the people. Scripture does not specifically say it, but this final outpouring of God's wrath not only has the worst earthquake the world has ever experienced, but it is also safe to say the worst hailstorm in the history of the world as well. With one-hundred-pound

hailstones there would be nowhere safe, and no building, if there are any left after the great earthquake, would stop these giant ice boulders. The only place that might be safe from this would be in a bomb shelter or a mountain cave, if any of these are intact after the greatest earthquake ever. It is likely the only people who will survive this hailstorm are the ones not struck by it. Those in military tanks might survive this hailstorm, but not for long because they are preparing to go to war with Almighty God. Now let's look at the Lord's return to the earth, found in *Revelation 19*.

REVELATION 19:11-14 (NKJV)

11 Now I saw heaven opened, and behold, a white horse. And He who sat on him was called Faithful and True, and in righteousness He judges and makes war.
12 His eyes were like a flame of fire, and on His head were many crowns. He had a name written that no one knew except Himself.
13 He was clothed with a robe dipped in blood, and His name is called The Word of God.
14 And the armies in heaven, clothed in fine linen, white and clean, followed Him on white horses.

It says He is coming to judge and make war and the armies of heaven are following Him. His redeemed people are part of the armies in heaven following Him, and that is made evident in *Revelation 17*.

REVELATION 17:12 (NKJV)

12 "The ten horns which you saw are ten kings who have received no kingdom as yet, but they receive authority for one hour as kings with the beast.

These are the ten horns of the beast-antichrist we learned about in *Revelation 13*.

REVELATION 17:13-14 (NKJV)

13 These are of one mind, and they will give their power and authority to the beast.
14 These will make war with the Lamb, and the Lamb will overcome them, for He is Lord of lords and King of kings;

and those who are with Him are called, chosen, and faithful."

Called, Chosen, and Faithful is a description of Christ's disciples. So, this passage is clear, the saints are with Christ when He returns to the earth and have been with Him since the Resurrection and Rapture at the Seventh Trumpet. As we learned from *Revelation 15*, the resurrected and Raptured saints witnessed the Bowl Judgments being poured out on the earth and are now returning to the earth with Christ. Now let's go back to *Revelation 19* and finish reading about Christ's return to the earth.

REVELATION 19:15-18 (NKJV)

[15] Now out of His mouth goes a sharp sword, that with it He should strike the nations. And He Himself will rule them with a rod of iron. He Himself treads the winepress of the fierceness and wrath of Almighty God.

[16] And He has on His robe and on His thigh a name written: King of kings and Lord of Lords.

[17] Then I saw an angel standing in the sun; and he cried with a loud voice, saying to all the birds that fly in the midst of heaven, "Come and gather together for the supper of the great God,

[18] that you may eat the flesh of kings, the flesh of captains, the flesh of mighty men, the flesh of horses and of those who sit on them, and the flesh of all people, free and slave, both small and great."

This passage leaves no doubt, the Lord is going to feed His enemies to the birds. A disgraceful end for the enemies of God.

REVELATION 19:19-21 (NKJV)

[19] And I saw the beast, the kings of the earth, and their armies, gathered together to make war against Him who sat on the horse and against His army.

[20] Then the beast was captured, and with him the false prophet who worked signs in his presence, by which he deceived those who received the mark of the beast and those who worshiped his image. These two were cast alive into the lake of fire burning with brimstone.

²¹ And the rest were killed with the sword which proceeded from the mouth of Him who sat on the horse. And all the birds were filled with their flesh.

The stage is set for the battle of Armageddon. The beast and his armies are gathered together to make war against Christ and His armies. The beast and the false prophet are captured and thrown alive into the lake of fire, still in their bodies, and the beast's armies are killed by the sword that comes out of the mouth of Christ. He is the Son of God and has all Power and Authority, even over the very breath they breathe. He breathed the very breath of life they have, so when He speaks His Word against them the breath of life in them will come out of their bodies and they are going to drop dead on the spot, no matter where they are at. The final statement of this passage says, *"And all the birds were filled with their flesh."*

The Lord also spoke of His return to the earth in the Gospels. Let's look at what He had to say there.

MATTHEW 24:37-41 (NKJV)
³⁷ But as the days of Noah were, so also will the coming of the Son of Man be.
³⁸ For as in the days before the flood, they were eating and drinking, marrying and giving in marriage, until the day that Noah entered the ark,
³⁹ and did not know until the flood came and took them all away, so also will the coming of the Son of Man be.
⁴⁰ Then two men will be in the field: one will be taken and the other left.
⁴¹ Two women will be grinding at the mill: one will be taken and the other left.

Jesus is comparing His return to the earth to Noah's flood, the worst Judgement of God in history, so far. Notice it says Noah's flood took them all away. As we continue to read this passage, it is making a comparison with what happened to those in Noah's Flood to the people taken away at His return. The people in Noah's Flood were taken away by the flood waters and were killed, so being taken away here is implying that they were involuntarily taken, just like the people in

Noah's time were taken away by the flood. So where are they being taken? *Matthew 24:28* tells us.

MATTHEW 24:28 (NKJV)
28 For wherever the carcass is, there the eagles will be gathered together.

A carcass is a dead body. Eagles gather to dead bodies to eat them, and just like in Jesus' comparison, the people taken away in Noah's time are killed and so are the people taken away when Jesus returns to the earth. There is further evidence of this in Scripture that we will look at to leave no doubt on this matter. This same message is taught by Jesus comparing His return to the days of Noah's Flood in the Gospel Luke, Jesus describes the same thing happening to the people taken away at His return. It also compares His return to the days of Lot and Sodom and Gomorra, and in all these accounts it says the people are killed. This entire account is found in *Luke 17:26-37*.

LUKE 17:26-27,34-37 (NKJV)
26 And as it was in the days of Noah, so it will be also in the days of the Son of Man:
27 They ate, they drank, they married wives, they were given in marriage, until the day that Noah entered the ark, and the flood came and destroyed them all.
34 I tell you, in that night there will be two men in one bed: the one will be taken and the other will be left.
35 Two women will be grinding together: the one will be taken and the other left.
36 Two men will be in the field: the one will be taken and the other left."
37 And they answered and said to Him, "Where, Lord?"
So He said to them, "Wherever the body is, there the eagles will be gathered together."

Just like in the Gospel of Matthew's account, the people being taken is compared to the days of Noah's Flood and they are taken away and killed. The Lord answers their question, wherever the body is the eagles will be gathered. We know from Matthew's account on this, these bodies are dead carcasses, and I can personally testify having lived in Montana for over ten years and seen many eagles, dead carcasses are

where eagles absolutely gather together.

REVELATION 19:17-18,21 (NKJV)

[17] Then I saw an angel standing in the sun; and he cried with a loud voice, saying to all the birds that fly in the midst of heaven, "Come and gather together for the supper of the great God,
[18] that you may eat the flesh of kings, the flesh of captains, the flesh of mighty men, the flesh of horses and of those who sit on them, and the flesh of all people, free and slave, both small and great."
[21] And the rest were killed with the sword which proceeded from the mouth of Him who sat on the horse. And all the birds were filled with their flesh.

All the people that are killed become part of the great supper of God, which is a feast for birds on the bodies of God's enemies. This is exactly what Jesus is teaching about on His return to the earth in the Gospels. His enemies are killed, and the eagles gather to eat their carcasses. Remember, the redeemed are already with the Lord. He is coming back to a hostile planet where most of the people have pledged allegiance to His arch enemy the beast, who is the antichrist. In fact, the Lord says in another place in the Gospels what He is going to do to His enemies who would not have Him as Lord and King when He returns.

LUKE 19:27 (NKJV)

[27] But bring here those enemies of mine, who did not want me to reign over them, and slay them before me.

Revelation 19 says the Lord is coming back to make war, but it also says He is coming back to judge.

REVELATION 19:11 (NKJV)

[11] Now I saw heaven opened, and behold, a white horse. And He who sat on him was called Faithful and True, and in righteousness He judges and makes war.

Not everyone is going to be in the armies that gather to fight in the battle of Armageddon. Those who are still alive after the battle of

Armageddon will be gathered to Christ for Judgment, and anyone with the mark of the beast will be killed and their bodies given to the birds for food. The final events on the earth that happen after the Rapture are in *Revelation 20*. We have looked at this passage, but this time we will focus on the events on the earth after the Rapture.

REVELATION 20:1-3 (NKJV)

¹ Then I saw an angel coming down from heaven, having the key to the bottomless pit and a great chain in his hand.
² He laid hold of the dragon, that serpent of old, who is the Devil and Satan, and bound him for a thousand years;
³ and he cast him into the bottomless pit, and shut him up, and set a seal on him, so that he should deceive the nations no more till the thousand years were finished. But after these things he must be released for a little while.

Satan, and I believe this includes all his demons, are bound for one-thousand years to give the nations of the earth a time when they are no longer deceived by the devil or ruled by him.

REVELATION 20:4-6 (NKJV)

⁴ And I saw thrones, and they sat on them, and judgment was committed to them. Then I saw the souls of those who had been beheaded for their witness to Jesus and for the word of God, who had not worshiped the beast or his image, and had not received his mark on their foreheads or on their hands. And they lived and reigned with Christ for a thousand years.
⁵ But the rest of the dead did not live again until the thousand years were finished. This is the first Resurrection.
⁶ Blessed and holy is he who has part in the first Resurrection. Over such the second death has no power, but they shall be priests of God and of Christ, and shall reign with Him a thousand years.

After Christ has defeated and judged the beast and all His enemies, and taken the earth back from Satan, He will reign with His people on the earth for one-thousand years. Scripture says in *2 Peter 3:8, "with the Lord one day is as a thousand years, and a thousand years as one day."* The Lord in Scripture, through the genealogies, has given

us the length of time of the different generations. We know it has been approximately two-thousand years since Christ and approximately four thousand-years from Adam to Christ, giving us approximately six-thousand years since Adam. So, in the context of one-thousand years being as one day in heaven's time, man has been on the earth for six days since creation. Since Christ's reign is one-thousand years, equivalent to one day in heaven's time, the one-thousand-year reign of Christ will be the seventh day, which is the sabbath day of rest. Since Satan is bound for one-thousand years and can no longer deceive and torment the earth, and the Lord Himself will be on the earth, it will experience a real sabbath rest. But as it says in *verse 3*, Satan will be loosed for a little while to test the people of the earth, a people who have not had to live by faith because the Lord Himself has been on the earth for one-thousand years. The few people who have survived the wrath of God and are still alive will repopulate the earth. This is revealed in *Zechariah 14*.

ZECHARIAH 14:16 (NKJV)

[16] And it shall come to pass that everyone who is left of all the nations which came against Jerusalem shall go up from year to year to worship the King, the Lord of hosts, and to keep the Feast of Tabernacles.

After the battle of Armageddon and Christ's judgement of the nations, those left alive will come up to Jerusalem to worship Christ every year. The following passage makes it very clear; The earth repopulates after the battle of Armageddon and Christ's judgement of the nations.

REVELATION 20:7-10 (NKJV)

[7] Now when the thousand years have expired, Satan will be released from his prison
[8] and will go out to deceive the nations which are in the four corners of the earth, Gog and Magog, to gather them together to battle, whose number is as the sand of the sea.
[9] They went up on the breadth of the earth and surrounded the camp of the saints and the beloved city. And fire came down from God out of heaven and devoured them.
[10] The devil, who deceived them, was cast into the lake of fire and brimstone where the beast and the false prophet

are. And they will be tormented day and night forever and ever.

After the one-thousand-year reign of Christ on the earth, Satan is released from his prison, which is the bottomless pit. He goes out to deceive everyone in the world that he can and then gathers them to battle Christ and the saints one last time. It says the number of those he gathers to battle Christ is as the sands of the sea. We know from the Great Tribulation that if the Lord did not shorten those days no flesh would survive, because the beast would kill everyone who would not worship his image and take his mark. Christ is going to execute everyone who has the mark of the beast, which would leave no human flesh, and this is exactly what would have happened if the Lord had not spared Noah and his family. The Lord spared Noah, and his family, to repopulate the earth, and He is going to spare some human lives so He can repopulate the earth after the Bowl Judgements. After the beast's reign of terror, and Christ executing everyone with the mark of the beast, there will be very few human beings in the flesh left alive. But, with one-thousand years with no war, and people living longer because Christ is on the earth, the earth is going to repopulate greatly. This is how Satan can gather an army with so many people it is like the sands of the sea from a world of very few people still alive after the return of Christ. After this, the last event in the history of the earth.

THE GREAT WHITE THRONE JUDGMENT

REVELATION 20:11-15 (NKJV)

[11] Then I saw a great white throne and Him who sat on it, from whose face the earth and the heaven fled away. And there was found no place for them.

[12] And I saw the dead, small and great, standing before God, and books were opened. And another book was opened, which is the Book of Life. And the dead were judged according to their works, by the things which were written in the books.

[13] The sea gave up the dead who were in it, and Death and Hades delivered up the dead who were in them. And they were judged, each one according to his works.

[14] Then Death and Hades were cast into the lake of fire. This is the second death.

[15] And anyone not found written in the Book of Life was cast into the lake of fire.

The Great White Throne Judgement is the second Resurrection and the judgement of the wicked. They will be judged by their works, and since they do not have the blood of the Lamb covering their sins, they will be cast into the lake of fire. Anyone not found in the Book of Life will be cast into the lake of fire. Everyone who died in sin before Christ came back to rule the earth will not be in the Book of Life. The few people who survive the wrath of God and live to repopulate the earth, if they become and stay loyal to Christ, their names would be in the Book of Life, and these would not be cast into the lake of fire. They will not experience the great blessings of those who lived by faith and were in the first Resurrection, but they will at least be saved and receive a reward for what they did for Christ. It would not be as great a reward as one who lived by faith, but the Lord is good and rewards all who serve Him.

A SUMMARY OF WHAT IS AFTER THE RAPTURE

The Judgment Seat of Christ

The Marriage Supper of the Lamb

The Seven Bowls of God's Wrath

Christ's Return to the Earth

The Battle of Armageddon

The Judgement of the Beast and False Prophet

The Judgement of those with the Mark of the Beast

The Great Supper of God where birds feast on the enemies of God

The Thousand Year Reign of Christ, Earth's Great Sabbath

The Final Battle between God and Satan

The Great White Throne Judgement where Satan, his demons and all
his followers are cast into the lake of fire forever

ABOUT THE AUTHOR

Christian Evangelist, born in Florida and raised in Maryland. Through a lifetime of learning and experiencing the Lord's work in his life in many different ways, he founded the ministry *Armed in Christ Ministries* with the goal of reaching the world with the truth about many key subjects of interest in our world today. He shares these messages through evangelism, Biblical truths, writing, and authentic prophetic messages and teachings. After receiving a dream from the Lord, he began working to create a book series to reveal the vision he had been given. Initially founded to spread the Gospel and prophetic messages about Heaven, Hell, and the End Times to the inner cities, Armed in Christ Ministries has grown as he ventures into a wide reach of spiritual teachings, theological studies, books, and videos to share the messages he founded it to share, on a larger stage. The ministries' first production, a book series to uncover the truth hidden in Scripture, the *"Whole Truth"* book series starting with *"The Whole Truth About the Rapture."*

SCRIPTURE INDEX

A

Acts 14:22 (NKJV)
Acts 24:14-15 (NKJV)

C

Colossians 3:11-12 (NKJV)
1 Corinthians 13:4-7 (NKJV)
1 Corinthians 15:23 (NKJV)
1 Corinthians 15:51-52 (NKJV)
2 Corinthians 12:2-4 (NKJV)

D

Daniel 11:30-37 (NKJV)
Daniel 12:1-13 (NKJV)
Daniel 2:41-43 (NIV)
Daniel 7:23-27 (NKJV)
Daniel 8:23-26 (NKJV)
Daniel 9:27 (NKJV)

E

Ephesians 1:13 (NKJV)
Ezekiel 14:19-20 (NKJV)

G

Genesis 19:17 (NKJV)
Genesis 19:26 (NKJV)
Genesis 37:9-10 (NKJV)
Genesis 6:9 (NKJV)

H

Hebrews 11:7 (NKJV)
Hebrews 11:35-40 (NKJV)
Hebrews 12:2 (NKJV)

J

John 3:16-17 (NKJV)

John 5:28-29 (NKJV)
John 15:13 (NKJV)
John 16:33 (NKJV)
1 John 2:15-18 (NKJV)
1 John 3:2-3 (NKJV)

L

Luke 9:23 (NKJV)
Luke 14:13-14 (NKJV)
Luke 17:24-27 (NKJV)
Luke 17:34-37 (NKJV)
Luke 19:27 (NKJV)
Luke 21:16-19 (NKJV)
Luke 21:34-36 (NKJV)

M

Mark 9:43 (NKJV)
Mark 13:11-14 (NKJV)
Mark 13:24-29 (NKJV)
Mark 16:19 (NKJV)
Matthew 5:8-12 (NKJV)
Matthew 5:39 (NKJV)
Matthew 6:24 (NKJV)
Matthew 10:28 (NKJV)
Matthew 13:27 (NKJV)
Matthew 18:8-9 (NKJV)
Matthew 24:3-9 (NKJV)
Matthew 24:10-30 (NKJV)
Matthew 24:31-51 (NKJV)
Matthew 25:1-10 (NKJV)
Matthew 26:52 (NKJV)
Matthew 27:52-53 (NKJV)
Matthew 23:29-31 (NKJV)

P

1 Peter 4:1-2 (NKJV)
1 Peter 4:12-14 (NKJV)
1 Peter 4:17-18 (KJV)

GLOSSARY

A

ABOMINATION OF DESOLATION

Statue; The image of the beast. The whole world will be commanded by the beast-antichrist to worship the Abomination of Desolation, the image of the beast.

B

BABYLON (PLACE)

A city; Starting as an ancient city in modern Iraq. Controls much of the wealth and commerce of the world and has great influence over the world. The nation that the Spirit of Babylon rules through and spreads all manner of sin throughout the world.

BABYLON (SPIRIT)

The spirit of Babylon; Does not die and is able to rise in power over and over again. Referred to as a feminine figure. Rules the world through greed, wealth, and sexual sin, and through the capital city or nation that rules other nations.

BEAT-ANTICHRIST

The beast, the antichrist, the son of perdition (hell). A great ruler, who through war...was mortally wounded and healed and who will gain control of the world through Satan and cause the Great Tribulation of the saints.

F

FALSE PROPHET

A second beast; Not the antichrist but promotes and forces the world to worship the beast-antichrist. Performs many signs and counterfeit operations of the Holy Spirit.

FINITE SPIRIT

A spirit of limited abilities.

M

MARK OF THE BEAST

A monetary mark; Those without the mark of the beast will be unable to buy or sell. Forced upon the world by the beast-antichrist in The Great Tribulation of the saints. Those who take the mark of the beast will be sealed to hell and will be killed when the Lord returns.

MARRIAGE SUPPER OF THE LAMB

An event after the Rapture; The saints dead and alive will be Resurrected and Raptured to meet the Lord in the air where after the Judgement, He will...

...take them to the wedding in heaven where Jesus will marry His bride, the Church.

R

RAPTURE

At the Seventh Trumpet, all the saints left alive on the earth are caught up to the Lord in the sky.

RESURRECTION

A power that only God Himself possesses. To raise someone from death to life, whether it be to their original body or to a new body.

RESURRECTION OF LIFE

A Resurrection of the saints; When the Lord returns at the Seventh Trumpet, all those who have died in Christ will be Resurrected and taken up to Him in the sky. The event alongside the Rapture. The first Resurrection.

RESURRECTION OF CONDEMNATION

A Resurrection of the wicked; Where those who have done evil will receive their judgment of condemnation at the end of the Trumpet Judgements.

T

TRIBULATION

A time of persecution and testing of the saints at any time in history, including in The Great Tribulation.

THE TRIBULATION

The final time of persecution and tribulation of the saints and can include The Great Tribulation.

THE GREAT TRIBULATION

The last three-and-a-half years when the beast-antichrist makes war with the saints and overcomes them and includes The Greatest Tribulation at the end of The Great Tribulation when the beast sets up his image the abomination of desolation and demands everyone worship the image or be executed.

THE GREATEST TRIBULATION

Part of The Great Tribulation and is near the end of it when the beast sets up his image the abomination of desolation and demands everyone worship the image or be executed.

Made in United States
North Haven, CT
22 November 2024